60

Spain. 1938. Oil on canvas, 36 x 23⅝ inches. Collection Edward James. The figures in the middle distance form the woman's head.

JAMES THRALL SOBY

SALVADOR DALI

THE MUSEUM OF MODERN ART

Reprint Edition, 1968. Published for The Museum of Modern Art by Arno Press

This reprinted edition was produced by the offset printing process. The text and plates were photographed separately from the original volume, and the plates rescreened. The paper and binding were selected to ensure the long life of this library grade edition.

Twelve thousand copies of this second revised edition have been printed in May 1946 for the Trustees of the Museum of Modern Art by the Carey Press. The color inserts have been printed by Wm. E. Rudge's Sons. Copyright 1946 by the Museum of Modern Art, New York. Printed in the United States of America.

Reprint Edition, 1968 Arno Press
Library of Congress Catalog Card No. 68-8368

CONTENTS

ACKNOWLEDGMENTS

I am greatly indebted to the artist and his wife and to the following persons for their generous help with this publication: Mr. Alfred H. Barr, Jr., Mr. Georges Keller, Mr. Julien Levy, Mr. A. Reynolds Morse, Mr. Beaumont Newhall, Mr. Monroe Wheeler, and Miss Lelia Wittler.

The extensive bibliography prepared by Mr. Bernard Karpel, Librarian of the Museum, has brought to light a great deal of material which has been utilized in revising the text relating to Dali's early career.

J. T. S.

TRUSTEES OF THE MUSEUM OF MODERN ART

SALVADOR DALI

SALVADOR DALI was born on May 11, 1904, at Figueras, a small town near Barcelona where his father was a notary and a leading citizen. Dali was educated first in a public school, later in the private academy in Figueras conducted by the Brothers of the Marist Order. By his own account his childhood was extraordinarily violent, marked by fits of hysteria and acts of rage toward his family and his playmates. The megalomania which he now considers one of his primary creative assets was apparent in youth: on several occasions he flung himself down a stone staircase in the schoolyard in order to savor the frightened attention of his classmates. He was abnormally imaginative and he matured under the strain of a hypersensitivity to his surroundings. Yet like so many artists of our century, he has remained deeply in love with his own childhood; its terrors and quick ecstasies are re-experienced time and again in the paintings he has created as an adult. As a painter he has never ceased to affirm his birthright and the environment in which he grew up. The high pitch of Spanish emotion with its Inquisitional heritage of cruelty and pain, the Catalan love of fantasy and sanctification of instinct, are unmistakably reflected in his works. Moreover, the locale of a majority of his paintings is Spanish, whether it is the flat glaring terrain of the landscape near Barcelona, the beach at Rosas, or the rocky gorges of the upper Catalan country.

Unlike his famous countryman, Picasso, Dali was not a precocious artist in the sense of having early evolved a consistently mature style of painting. At twenty-two, an age at which Picasso had already begun to turn his back on the professional competence of his Blue Period, Dali was still attending the School of Fine Arts in Madrid and had not yet decided what direction his art would take. Nevertheless, he had already been painting seriously for a long period and had passed through an astonishing series of artistic phases. Before he was ten years old he had completed two oil paintings, *Joseph greeting his brethren* and *Portrait of Helen of Troy,* ambitious subjects for a child, to say the least. Both paintings were executed in the style of the nineteenth-century painters of genre scenes. The fact is interesting in view of Dali's later profession of respect for artists like Meissonier. It seems significant, too, that in reply to a question as to which Spanish painters he had admired most as a young man, Dali replied, "Modesto Urgell and Mariano Fortuny." He described the first of these two artists as "the Catalan Böcklin," the second as "the inventor of anecdotal colorism and the Meissonier of our country." Apparently even as a youth he felt a decided preference for those artists who had put a precise technique to story-telling purpose. It was a preference which was finally to bring him into sharp opposition to Picasso's generation, which had attempted to banish literature and history from the subject matter of painting.

During his adolescence Dali experimented with Impressionism and Pointillism, having been influenced by an exhibition of late nineteenth-century French art held at Barcelona and by the Impressionist paintings of the Spaniard, Ramon Pichot. The period of his interest in Impressionism and its later ramifications was of relatively short duration, and by the time

3

he became a student in the Madrid School of Fine Arts in 1921 he was in full and characteristically violent reaction against his own previous enthusiasm. On one occasion, when a student, he is said to have shown his contempt for the Impressionist tradition by winning a wager that he could paint a prize-winning Pointillist picture by splashing paint at a canvas from a distance of three feet. On another occasion when he and his classmates were told to look at a Gothic statue of the Virgin and paint exactly what they saw, Dali executed a picture of a pair of scales. To his irate teacher he explained, "Perhaps you see a Virgin like everyone else. I see a pair of scales" (bibl. 96). Thus were evinced in youth two qualities which largely account for the exceptional fame his art has since earned him: his technical virtuosity; and his insistence on painting the counter-appearances suggested to him by what he now calls his "paranoiac" processes of thought.

Around 1920 Dali's parents, returning from a visit to Paris, brought with them a catalog and manifesto of Italian Futurist art. Presumably these publications had been issued in Paris or Milan just prior to the World War, when Futurist activity had reached its climax. After perusing them Dali turned to the solution of the problems posed by the Futurist doctrine, using a technique in which traces of his earlier absorption in Pointillism still lingered. He was probably especially fascinated by the Futurists' attempts to suggest simultaneously various aspects of objects in motion, since these attempts are more than distantly related to his own preoccupation with multiple appearances of the same object. In Dali's case, as will presently be seen, the basis of interest in simultaneity has been psychological rather than kinetic, as it was among the Futurists. Yet the Futurists, no less than he, were intent upon amplifying tangible reality and proposed transfigurations in subject matter which presupposed an abnormal perception.

From an interest in Futurism Dali progressed, from 1923 to 1925, to an interest in the *scuola metafisica,* the "Metaphysical School," founded by Giorgio de Chirico and Carlo Carrà in Ferrara in 1915-1916. The art of the *scuola* was extremely well known in Barcelona, primarily through Mario Broglio's magazine, *Valori Plastici,* issued from Rome during the years 1919-1921. Indeed in Catalan circles devoted to advanced art the work of de Chirico, Carrà and Giorgio Morandi was discussed almost as intensively as that of the leading figures in the School of Paris.

Dali's exposure to the art of the *scuola metafisica* was of paramount importance in his early career. The school's doctrine was eventually to swerve him from the abstract approach of the Cubist-Futurist tradition toward the Surrealist movement's concern with man's psychology. For the *scuola metafisica* had directly prefigured the reaction against purely abstract art which Surrealism in general and Dali in particular were to exemplify so forcefully. It had rejected Cubism as merely a late development of French Naturalism, concerned only with a plastic rearrangement of external appearances rather than with a reappraisal of these appearances. It had strongly opposed Futurism's ideological dependence on the concrete aspects of contemporary civilization; it had refuted Futurism's preoccupation with machines and machine-forms, an engrossing fact in view of Dali's later contempt for the industrialism of the twentieth century. The movement had proposed to explore the deeper roots of man's

4

existence, to create an art of metaphysical incantation arising from inner perception and experience. It had emphasized the artist's salvation through philosophical speculation, his comfort in the enigma, his retreat to the dream. However important the differences between its program and that of Surrealism, there can be no question that Dali was prepared for his career as a Surrealist by his eager adoption of the tenets of *pittura metafisica*.

These tenets were in essence a rationalization of the art which the school's greatest figure, Giorgio de Chirico, had achieved in the five years before the school had come into being. But oddly enough, considering the preponderant influence which de Chirico was later to have upon him, Dali at this time emulated Carrà's art more closely. During the years 1923-1925 he executed several still lifes which owe more to Carrà's technique than to that of de Chirico. They are marked by an emotive archaism peculiar to the former rather than to the latter as may be seen in the *Still life* of 1924 here reproduced (page 29). Traces of his interest in *pittura metafisica* were to persist in his works of a slightly later date; the fish in the foreground of his *Neo-Cubist Academy* (page 32) clearly derive from de Chirico's *Sacred Fish* of 1915, a picture reproduced in *Valori Plastici* and greatly revered by such proto-Surrealists as Max Ernst.

In 1924 Dali was suspended from the Madrid School of Fine Arts for a year on a charge of inciting the students to insurrection against the School authorities. During part of this year he was also briefly imprisoned at Figueras and Gerona for political activity against the government. He returned to the Madrid School of Fine Arts for a time but was expelled permanently in October, 1926, presumably on the grounds of extravagant personal behavior. Meanwhile, in 1925, he had begun to exhibit with the *Sociedad de Artistos Ibéricos* in Madrid and at the Gallery Dalmau in Barcelona. He was beginning to achieve considerable local fame as a leading Catalan painter of the young generation. His works of 1925-1927 were frequently discussed and reproduced in the Catalan magazine, *L'Amic de les Arts,* for which Dali himself wrote a number of articles (see bibl.).

During this same period, 1925-1927, Dali worked alternately in two distinct styles: realistic and abstract, or "objective" and "cubist," as they were described by *L'Amic de les Arts'* critic, M. A. Cassanyes. Thus in 1925 he made a careful drawing indicating the naturalistic laws of lighting and perspective to be followed in his painting, *Girl sewing* (page 30). The picture's objective clarity of statement and precision of technique relate it to the tradition of Dutch seventeenth century realism, a tradition to which *The basket of bread* (page 30), painted the same year, is even more closely allied. Dali already felt that veneration for Vermeer which was to have so lasting an effect on his own art. In 1927, in *L'Amic de Les Arts,* he wrote of the Dutch master: "In the history of visual perception, his eyes furnish the highest example of probity."

At the same time, however, Dali was swayed in quite another direction by the influence of our own century's Cubist revolution, as may be seen in the *Harlequin* of late 1925 or early 1926 (page 29). Remembering that Picasso was a fellow Spaniard, it is understandable that Dali should have been caught at some point by the immense suction of his ideas, and as he himself put the matter in his *Secret Life of Salvador Dali,* "I was supremely conscious of one through cubism in order to get it out of my system once and for all, and erhaps I could at least learn to draw!" In 1926, however, he at some point both seventeenth-century realism and analytical Cubism toward a monu- le quite obviously based on Picasso's post-Cubist compositions of 1924. motifs in such a Picasso as the famous *Red Tablecloth* of 1924 and the still life of 1926, here reproduced (page 31), are very similar. But Dali's handling is more agitated than Picasso's and the upper sections of his canvas abound in references to the Italian *pittura metafisica* as well as to Picasso's ballet décors of 1919-1921.

. At this same date, 1926, Dali was also influenced by Picasso's Neo-Classic style of the earlier 1920s. The influence is apparent in the *Neo-Cubist Academy* (page 32) which is, indeed, a synthesis of various Picassean styles: Cubism in the foreground; ponderous Greco-Roman figures; post-Cubist abstraction of still-life elements. But having erected this fairly serene eclectic world, Dali was almost immediately impelled to do it psychological violence, as may be seen in *Figures on the sand* (page 32). In this work we come upon plain signs of a proto-Surrealism. The violently foreshortened figures are sprawled in strange postures on a Cubist plain which stretches deep to the sea; the shadows are dramatic and unreal; the faceted cliffs are the boundaries of a dream-image; the background objects diminish weirdly. And if the figures still derive from Picasso's Neo-Classicism, their setting attests Dali's continuing regard for the counter-reality envisioned by the *scuola metafisica*.

In 1927 Dali completed *Blood is sweeter than honey* (page 33); its title's derivation is explained at some length on page 183 of his *Secret Life*. The picture marks an extraordinary progression away from the realism, Cubism, post-Cubism and Neo-Classicism of the previous year, toward that art of subconscious obsessions which his mature work was to become. The painting contains a wide range of the fantastic symbols so often depicted in later years. Taken in conjunction with a few other 1927 works of comparable intention, notably the *Apparatus and hand* (page 33), it must be read as a forecast of what we now know as the Dalinian style. Its rather special intensity may come from the fact that it was probably a naively compulsive expression, not yet a product of the fixed program of anti-reason which he was to develop in 1929, with the moral support of the Parisian Surrealists.

Sometime during 1928 Dali made a brief excursion to Paris, where he met Picasso. Prompted, perhaps, by his great countryman's lack of reverence for traditional media and inspired by the latter's *collages,* he returned home to execute several huge abstract canvases from which stones and all manner of heavy objects were suspended by thick cords. A few months later he returned to Paris for a second visit, during which he met and came under the influence of Miro, was introduced to Robert Desnos and Paul Eluard of the Surrealist group, and signed a contract with the Goemans Gallery for an exhibition which he went home to prepare. For several months after his return to Spain he continued to work at abstractions on which the imprint of Miro's personality gradually superseded that of Picasso. This short period marks the last phase of Dali's interest in abstract art. Presently he was to react violently against this kind of art in general. By 1935 his book, *Conquest of the Irrational,* was to appear, containing a chapter entitled, "The Abject Misery of Abstraction-

6

Creation." The chapter was to include the phrase, "this model mental debility called abstract art."

The signs of Dali's permanent defection from the abstract movement were obvious by the summer of 1929. By then he had definitely decided to apply what he knew to be an extraordinary manual dexterity to the exact transcription on canvas of his subconscious thoughts and dreams. By midsummer he had found his stride, painting *The lugubrious game* and *Accommodations of desire* (page 35). When his paintings began to arrive in Paris, it was clear that his sympathies lay with the Surrealists. A few weeks before his exhibition opened at the Goemans Gallery, André Breton, Surrealism's central figure, agreed to write the foreword to his catalog. On hearing Dali's decision to come to Paris to live, Breton appointed him an official Surrealist. Within a short time Dali was to become the movement's most spectacular exponent.

It was not the painter's technical gifts alone which won him prominence, although the draftsmanship in *Studies* (page 83) or the brushwork in *The feeling of becoming* (page 38) would probably earn an artist attention in any epoch. What distinguished him from established artists within the Surrealist group was his bringing to Surrealist art a new objectivity to replace the confessional subjectivity of his predecessors. He did so by changing the formula of creative stimulus. Whereas the art of the earlier Surrealists had often sprung from an artificially induced and terminable state of receptivity to subconscious inspiration, Dali declared that his art sprang from a constant, hallucinatory energy. He proposed to paint like a madman rather than as an occasional somnambulist. He added that the only difference between himself and a madman was that he was not mad. But by simulating madness he professed himself able at will to proclaim the unreasonable with extreme conviction because his reason could be made to lose its power of objection. He made his purpose clear in his first book, *La femme visible,* published in 1930. "I believe the moment is at hand," he then wrote, "when by a paranoiac and active advance of the mind, it will be possible (simultaneously with automatism and other passive states) to systemize confusion and thus to help discredit completely the world of reality."

The history of art can furnish almost continuous precedent for Dali's reverence for madness, the most recent example being that of the nineteenth-century Romantic artists who endowed the deranged mind with special allure. Yet there is a cardinal difference between Dali's attitude toward insanity and that of a Romantic like Géricault. Whereas Géricault had regarded madness as a phenomenon which was exotic precisely because it was impenetrable, Dali regarded it as an ideal state, to be entered into by the artist himself. He seems to have had no fear that, having identified himself with madness, his communication of its mysteries would be limited to the insane or to those with a scientific knowledge of insanity. In his *Declaration of the Independence of the Imagination and the Rights of Man to His Own Madness,* he later wrote: ". . . all men are equal in their madness . . . madness (visceral cosmos of the subconscious) constitutes the common base of the human spirit."

Of Dali's early attempts at communicating his "paranoiac" visions, *Accommodations of desire* and *Illumined pleasures* (page 34) are typical and excellent examples. Both owe to

De Chirico: *The Sailors' Barracks.* 1914.
Collection Henry Clifford.

De Chirico's pioneer use of deep perspective, sharp mysterious shadows, and evocative grouping of enigmatic or incongruous objects, influenced Dali in such works as those reproduced on pages 29, 34, 35, 36, 52 and 57.

Giorgio de Chirico an ideological debt which they share with nearly all Surrealist art. In neither picture is the technical influence of de Chirico so direct as in other paintings of the years 1929-1931, such as *The invisible man* (page 36), *Simulacrum of night* and *Vertigo*, yet this influence is nonetheless unmistakable in both. It was de Chirico who had reaffirmed deep perspective as a poetic instrument at a time when the Cubists were dismissing the third dimension as illusory or were representing it through a calligraphic shorthand. In *Accommodations of desire* and *Illumined pleasures* Dali has utilized the recessive planes, abrupt scaling down of background objects and elongation of shadows through which, from 1911 to 1915, de Chirico had given his paintings of Italian squares an almost *trompe l'oeil* depth. Moreover Dali has borrowed from de Chirico an anti-naturalist manipulation of light to suggest the atmosphere of hallucination or dreams. In *Illumined pleasures* he has further adopted de Chirico's device of the boxed painting-within-the-painting, using it as a method of presenting successive aspects of dream imagery.

Here the resemblance between de Chirico's early paintings and those of Dali ends. For while de Chirico's art was basically concerned with a broad idealization of the process of dreaming, Dali's presented the scenario of a given "paranoiac" dream; while de Chirico had evoked the sensation of somnambulism in terms of lyric experience, Dali illustrated the details of a specific dream-continuity at a climax of its terrifying activity. In 1913 de Chirico had written: "What I hear is worth nothing; there is only what I see with my eyes open and, even more, what I see with them closed." But what he had seen with his eyes closed had been the squares of Italy, arbitrarily transformed in accordance with the inner dictates of his inspiration, often ominous but always noble, elegiac and restrained. When Dali closed his eyes, it was to see a turbulent procession of images, indicative of all manner of psychic disturbance. Having read Freud with furious enthusiasm, he was no longer content, as de Chirico had been, to state the workings of the subconscious in general poetic terms. Instead he wished to document these workings in full detail and with scientific accuracy. He was already what he afterwards declared all artists must become, "[a] carnivorous fish . . . swimming between two kinds of water, the cold water of art and the warm water of science" (bibl. 56).

Despite his belief in the constant inspirational force of his "paranoia," Dali shared the group Surrealist faith in sleep as an aid in distracting the vigil of conscious reason. Sleep, as he has since made clear in the canvas by that name (page 62), was to him a monster, because in their dreams men are free to commit the most hideous crimes; sleep was embryonic, because it gives men the warm shelter and immunity of the womb. Yet if a number of his early paintings are literal transcriptions of dreams, he nevertheless frequently relied on the waking inspiration of his "paranoiac" thought. He did so by recording the first image which occurred to him and then filling in the picture space with images suggested by this first image. Just as a true paranoiac is constantly seeing countless persecutory forms in whatever object is presented to his view, so Dali claimed that any given image suggested endless other images to him because of his "paranoiac" sensitivity. Applied to his painting, this theory meant that once his subconscious had supplied an initial form the task of elaboration could be entrusted to conscious paranoiac reasoning. He defined the matter in *La femme visible* as follows: "The images which paranoiac thought may suddenly release will not merely spring from the unconscious; the force of their paranoiac power will itself be at the service of the unconscious."

Whether inspired by dreams or active paranoiac reasoning, Dali's paintings continued the restoration of the anecdote to art which the Dadaist works of Duchamp, Picabia and Max Ernst had initiated. He thus helped revive the theory of painting as an illustrative medium against which the Cubists had fought so relentlessly. (Following the lead of de Chirico and Ernst, he gave, and still gives, long descriptive titles to his paintings by contrast with the bare nomenclature of Cubist works.) The form which the anecdote took in his works was, of course, Freudian—that is, it was expressed in terms of symbolic appearances emerging from the dim, relatively unexplored regions of the subconscious. But in restoring the anecdote, whatever its form, Dali was obliged to face the limitation of all story-telling art: its tendency to become outmoded through later reactions against the literary, scientific or historical documentation which it has undertaken.

Dali proposed to transcend this limitation by the force of his revelations and by the precision with which he communicated them. He brought to the task an extremely fertile imagination which Picasso said reminded him of "an outboard motor continually running" (bibl. 171), and a clarity of technique already exhibited in *The basket of bread* of 1926. He called his technique "handmade photography," by which he meant to say that it defined appearances so sharply as to make them rival those which, recorded by the camera, were indubitably existent. With him, in however temporary a sense, came to an end the reaction against painting as a photographic medium which had gathered force throughout the late nineteenth century and reached a climax in the early twentieth. Whereas André Derain, in describing his career as a Fauve, had written, "this was the epoch of photography . . . a fact which counted in our reaction against everything which resembled negatives taken from life," Dali went so far as to give his paintings a surface similar to that of glossy photographic prints. He wished, in a word, to depict the unreal with such extreme realism that its truth and validity could no longer be questioned.

In certain of his early canvases, among them *Accommodations of desire,* he adopted the Cubist practice of affixing real substances, or photographs and engravings of them, to his canvases. He did not do so in order to establish a link with reality, as the Cubists had done. Instead he intended to set the key for an over-all pattern of exactitude. Thus, in some of his early paintings, pasted-on engravings and photographs are supplemented by painted replicas so carefully executed as to be indistinguishable from the originals. In other pictures of the period, such as *Illumined pleasures,* forms are so painstakingly rendered as to startle the observer into a belief in the existence of the phenomena recorded. Just as ships within bottles have exaggerated identities as ships, because of their having been laboriously erected within so confined a space, so the objects in Dali's paintings were intended to have an added wonder because of their diminutive scale and completeness of detail.

At this juncture in his career Dali declared himself totally uninterested in the esthetic values of color and line, thus taking his place in the anti-artistic cycle which had begun so violently with the Dadaists. As already briefly noted, he admired painters of the past, particularly Meissonier, whose art was almost wholly notable for its photographic clarity of technique. He claimed to be completely indifferent to richness of pigment or elegance of contour. He not infrequently used offensive combinations of color; he often deliberately painted in the flat, unimaginative tones which popular artists employ in imitation of hand-tinted prints. In *Conquest of the Irrational* he gave his reasons for so doing. "The illusionism of the most abjectly *arriviste* and irresistible imitative art, the usual paralysing [sic] tricks of *trompe l'oeil,* the most analytically narrative and discredited academicism," he wrote, "can all become sublime hierarchies of thought and the means of approach to new exactitudes of concrete irrationality." What alone interested him was the quality of his obsessions and the means of their literal transcription. "My whole ambition in the pictorial domain," as he put the matter, "is to materialize the images of concrete irrationality with the most imperialist fury of precision" (bibl. 56).

In the above-mentioned paintings of 1929 and in other outstanding canvases of that year —*The lugubrious game, Portrait of Paul Eluard, The first days of spring*—occur many of the iconographical devices which were to haunt his art for many years. The foetal creature which lies in the foreground of *The persistence of memory* (page 39) begins as the profile of a woman in both *Illumined pleasures* and *The lugubrious game.* In the two last-named paintings, as in a majority of his early works, appears the female praying mantis, an insect endeared to the artist by its habit of devouring the male immediately following the act of procreation. The pictures in general are crowded with implements of persecution, particularly with sharp instruments symbolic of mutilation; they swarm with fetishes direct from Krafft-Ebing's case histories—slippers, keys, hair and so on. They are, moreover, largely concerned with what Dali called the three cardinal images of life: excrement, blood and putrefaction. Those who object to them on the grounds that they are scatologic, sacrilegious and ugly, would hear no dissent from Dali himself. "It has to be said once and for all to art critics, artists &c.," he wrote, "that they need expect nothing from the new Surrealist images but disappointment, distaste and repulsion" (bibl. 52). In painting these images he was attempting to release the dark, repressed poetry of the subconscious. He had previously accepted without reservation André Breton's definition of Surrealism as "thought's dictation, all exercise of reason and every esthetic or moral preoccupation being absent."

Shortly after his arrival in Paris Dali evolved what he later called "the paranoiac-critical method" and defined as a "spontaneous method of irrational knowledge based upon the interpretative-critical association of delirious phenomena" (bibl. 56). Reduced to simpler terms, the method consisted in a critical approach to accepted truths and appearances which substituted for the traditional concept of their meaning a new concept, often diametrically opposite and based primarily on psychological research. Thus far the method is clearly Freudian in inspiration. But to Freud's system of dispassionate psychoanalysis, Dali added an implemental force which he considered his own: his ability spontaneously to recognize hidden, associated meanings because of his "paranoiac" sensitivity. He presently began to apply the method to the sanctified and the obvious, and to probe for evidence of a reverse meaning long concealed from normal vision. The results of his scrutiny were immediately reflected in his painting.

The first of the several thematic obsessions which the "paranoiac-critical method" led him to record was concerned with the legend of William Tell. In accordance with his "paranoiac-critical" standards of interpretation, the legend was drastically re-read. It became not a legend of filial devotion, but one of incestuous mutilation, and as René Crevel wrote in *Dali ou l'anti-obscurantisme,* "As Freud resuscitated Oedipus, he (Dali) resuscitated William Tell." Dali utilized his interpretation of the legend for the libretto of a ballet, published in his book, *Babaouo,* in 1932. Beginning in 1930 with *William Tell* and ending in 1934 with the large panel, *The enigma of William Tell,* the legend supplied the subject for a number of his most important paintings, among them *The old age of William Tell* (page 41), one of the finest works of his career. In these paintings the subject of mutilation is treated in varying degrees of symbolic disguise. The theme itself is embroidered with a frieze of objects which had become obsessive for the artist: fried eggs on a platter, limp watches, swarming ants and so on.

A second and equally lasting thematic obsession reflected in his art was supplied by his reappraisal of Millet's famous painting, *The Angelus,* as a monument to sexual repression. To Dali's mind the picture's pious subject matter served merely as an outer disguise to a vicious, instinctive energy which he considered truly poetic. Like the other Surrealists he preferred passion to restraint, desire to its sublimation, the black, erotic power of the subconscious to the cool equivocation of reason. Not unmindful that *The Angelus* was widely

11

Art nouveau forms which influenced Dali in such pictures as *The invisible man* (page 36) and *The font* (page 37). *Left:* Ornament from entrance to Paris subway, 1900. *Right: art nouveau* bust. Both from Dali: *De la beauté terrifiante et comestible de l'architecture 'modern' style* (bibl. 10).

regarded as a sacred image, he used its bowed figures as symbols of a furious counter-reality concealed from normal vision by a superficially devout iconography. The *Angelus* figures appear in a number of his paintings executed between 1932 and 1935, among them those here reproduced on pages 45 and 56. He also included the figures in concrete reconstructions of dream imagery which he called "Surrealist objects operating symbolically." Following the line of Freud's research on the hidden forms in Leonardo's *Virgin on the lap of Saint Ann,* he explored what he considered to be the erotic origin of Millet's inspiration in general (bibl. 72).

Meanwhile, his art was affected by more purely esthetic influences. Certain of Max Ernst's poetic devices impressed him and in 1930 his painting drew close to that of the young French Surrealist, Yves Tanguy. In *The font* (page 37) the ball-like forms on the marble floor suggest Tanguy's curious images, while the general tonality has the shimmering iridescence of the latter's works of this period. Moreover, the tilted, broad perspective of Dali's canvas, scattered with minute objects which cast heavy shadows, is closely allied to that in such Tanguy paintings as the Museum of Modern Art's *Mama, Papa is wounded!* of 1927. Tanguy had in turn inherited his interest in deep perspective from de Chirico, but he had used perspective in a manner which, by comparison with that of de Chirico, was rather more abstract and more freely atmospheric. Dali followed Tanguy's example. In his paintings of 1930 and 1931 space is manipulated to suggest an infinity against which the drama of his objects and figures is projected. Yet the objects themselves, with exceptions such as the object on the ground in *Shades of night descending* (page 42), are usually readily identifiable, while those of Tanguy are not. From the meeting of Psychoanalysis and Morphology, later celebrated in one of Dali's canvases (page 70), Psychoanalysis had already emerged triumphant.

The influence of Tanguy was supplemented by that of *art nouveau* architecture and decoration. Having expressed a dislike for abstract art, Dali also dismissed modern architecture in favor of what he was presently to call the "undulant-convulsive" style which had been evolved at the end of the previous century (bibl. 60). He came by this preference more or less naturally. In Catalan Spain he had been surrounded by the architectural fantasies of the style's most astonishing practitioner, Antoni Gaudì. Indeed, it seems safe to assume that Dali's enthusiastic familiarity with Gaudì's works had been a determining factor in his decision to become himself a champion of the irrational and the fantastic. Certainly it now prompted his contempt for what he described as the "hyper-materialism" of contemporary architecture as this architecture had been defined by Le Corbusier, Gropius, Oud, Miës van der Rohe and their disciples. Dali was not, of course, the only artist in Paris to avow this distaste, since the younger Surrealists and the Neo-Romantic artists shared his feeling, while Picasso, Matisse and other leaders of the older generation had been apathetic toward the achievements of even the greatest modern architects. Yet Dali was more extreme in his belief than any of these men, and perhaps the only one capable of saying, "For one thing is certain: I hate simplicity in all its forms" (bibl. 56). He was also the first, as he later pointed out, to take *art nouveau* architecture seriously as an antidote to contemporary building. (He took it so seriously, in fact, that he wished to pursue his identification with it to the point of eating it.) The degree of his isolation from the esthetic theory then current may be measured by the fact that in 1929, the year of his arrival in Paris, a magazine of advanced Parisian taste, *Cahiers d'Art,* had described Gaudì as the architect who had utterly ruined the city of Barcelona.

The influence of *art nouveau* architecture and ornamentation on Dali's art was a broad one and profoundly affected his visual habits, especially during the years 1930-1934. Many of the ectoplasmic forms which haunt his works of this period are based upon the "undulant-convulsive" style of *art nouveau* decorative busts or of the ornamentation of the Paris subway stations and of Gaudì's façades in Barcelona, as may be seen in *The font.* Although the influence cannot often be so directly traced and segregated, it largely accounts for the metal torso and its appendages in *Javanese mannequin* (page 47). In the few sculptures which Dali executed during this period, among them *Hysterical and aerodynamic feminine nude* of 1934, he appears to have been inspired equally by *art nouveau* forms and by the Futurist sculpture of Boccioni, for which he has on several occasions expressed a deep admiration.

From the beginning of his career Dali has evaded questions as to the meaning of his paintings by stating that he does not know what their meaning is. No one, he adds, is more astonished by the images which appear on his canvases than he; and having created them, he feels that his responsibility toward them is ended. Nevertheless his writings at times furnish partial data on the iconography of certain paintings, as in the case of *The persistence of memory* (page 39) and *The spectre of sex appeal* (page 48). Of the former picture he has written, with a glance at Einstein which the great physicist has not yet returned: "be persuaded that Salvador Dali's famous limp watches are nothing else than the tender, extravagant and solitary paranoiac-critical camembert of time and space" (bibl. 56). Although precisionists in psychological discussion may find the sentence equivocal, to put it mildly, the word "camembert" furnishes a clue to one of the painter's most fervid obsessions—his preoccupation with malleability, his passion for *softness,* which leads him to convert hard objects, like watches, into substances as soft as camembert. Furthermore, in *La femme visible* he had previously written that rotting flesh covered with ants could have "the hard and blinding flash of new gems," were it not for the intervention of one's awareness of time. In *The persistence of memory* time has gone limp, and the ants on the watch in the foreground have the glitter of rare jewels.

The ideological inspiration for *The spectre of sex appeal* has also been described in part by the artist. "I am very proud," he wrote, "of having predicted in 1928, at the height of the cult for functional and practical anatomy, in the midst of the most shocking scepticism, the imminence of the round and salivary muscles of Mae West, viscous and terrible with hidden biological meanings. Today I announce that all the new sexual allure of women will come from the possible utilization of their capacities and resources as ghosts, that is to say, their possible dissociation, their charnel and luminous decomposition" (bibl. 80). He added that the woman with sex appeal would henceforth be demountable as the figure in *The spectre of sex appeal* quite clearly is, so that she could satisfy her profound exhibitionism by detaching various sections of her anatomy and passing them around to be admired separately. It has also been his conviction that bones should be worn outside rather than beneath the flesh, a conviction absolutely opposed to that of one of his idols, Ingres, who was so terrified of bones that he was at pains to cover them with ample flesh and almost to deny their structural function in anatomy. Dali consequently conceived of the ghost of sex appeal as composed of protruding bones and stuffed, detachable forms held in place by crutches which he defined in the *Dictionnaire abrégé du surréalisme* as "wooden supports deriving from Cartesian philosophy. Generally used as a support for the tenderness of soft structures." The ghost is painted in more brilliant colors than he had ever before used, because it must be "more beautiful and terrifying than the white truffle of death: a rainbow" (bibl. 80).

Dali's preoccupation with bones reached a climax in 1933 and 1934 when he executed a series of paintings in which all manner of bone distortions, chiefly cephalic, are exhaustively treated. The inspiration for the series may have come from a childhood memory of a man suffering from hydrocephalus. It is surely no mere coincidence, however, that for several years prior to 1933, Picasso had been engrossed by osseous formations and deformations. Since Dali's arrival in Paris his respect for his compatriot had steadily become more pronounced. By 1933 Picasso was on intimate terms with the Surrealists, and since his latest works were the subject of almost daily discussion among them, it seems reasonable to suppose that Dali's bone series was at least partially inspired by that of Picasso. Whatever their derivation, *Myself at the age of ten when I was the grasshopper child* (page 43) and *Average atmosphero-cephalic bureaucrat in the act of milking a cranial harp* (page 49) are key examples of a series which reached its high point in *The invisible, fine and average harp*. It is perhaps unnecessary to point out that Dali's preoccupation with harps is in part motivated by his admiration for Harpo Marx, of whom he has made many drawings (page 86).

There is evidence that Dali's contempt for purely esthetic values in painting had begun to weaken by late 1933. *The phantom cart* (page 44) of that year was succeeded in 1934, 1935 and 1936 by the series of beach scenes at Rosas which included *Paranoiac-astral image* (page 55) and *Noon* (page 58). All three of the above-named pictures are notable for a new and deliberate lyricism; all are luminous in tone, their subtle gradations of color a far cry from the hard cacophony of "handmade photography." Yet the change they illustrate is not one of technique alone. By comparison with *The spectre of sex appeal* these paintings reveal that the artist could sometimes abandon his ideological dramatics to attain a more dulcet poesy. He obviously did so only temporarily, since in 1936 he was to paint *Soft construction with boiled beans; premonition of civil war* (page 61), possibly the most savage and relent-lessly psychopathic of all his works. But for a time, at least, he was content to record a quieter inspiration. In *The phantom cart,* the contours of the wagon merge with those of the town toward which it is traveling, so that by an appealing, poetic *tour de force* the cart becomes its own destination. In paintings of the Rosas series, too, sentiment is granted a new importance. Returning to the seashore which he had visited in youth, Dali painted the series of pictures, relatively free of Freudian connotation, in which the central figures are those of himself as a child and of his childhood nurse.

Apart from *Paranoiac-astral image* and *Noon,* the series included, among other paintings, *Apparition on the beach at Rosas* and *Paranoiac-medianimic image.* Dali described the figures in all these pictures as "instantaneous," by which he meant that they were intended to have the hallucinatory appearance of stereoscopic images projected briefly against a prepared background. Precisely what stimulated the artist's interest in figures of the kind is difficult to say, although precedent for his interest may certainly be found. Nearly a hundred years before, Gustave Courbet had given certain of his figures a weirdly fleeting connection with the landscape, a procedure which led Giorgio de Chirico to declare that Courbet's figures "do not appear in their current guise (verism), but in their poetic and phantasmal aspect (realism)." Perhaps following Courbet's example, Christian Bérard in 1933 painted a series of beach scenes in which a sense of dislocation between the figures and the landscape is purposely conveyed for phantomic effect. But while Bérard's influence on Dali has become recognizable in very recent years, there is no reason to suppose that it was felt as early as 1934-1936. Moreover, perhaps the nearest equivalent to Dali's "instantaneous" figures is not to be found in the art of either Courbet or Bérard, but in that of the Englishman, William Dyce, whose *Pegwell Bay* (1858) Dali could not have seen at that time. Dali did not go to England until after his Rosas series was well begun, and even then was almost exclusively preoccupied with the Pre-Raphaelites, whose works he found "paranoiac" in every detail (bibl. 97). It therefore seems likely that he was impelled to paint his series by the simple fact of his having spent a vacation at Rosas where figures appeared like ghosts in the brilliant seashore light. A painter of original and highly personal vision, Dali has seldom had to go beyond his own feverish imagination for inspiration. The point must be emphasized here, lest a discussion of parallels between his art and that of other painters be taken to signify that he has been an imitative or eclectic artist. Whatever accusations may be brought against him, this one surely cannot be among them. On the contrary, his individuality is so pronounced that its effect on present-day esthetics is widely discernible, surviving drastic adaptation and dilution at the hands of lesser artists.

Although the costumes worn by the figures in the Rosas series can probably be ascribed to the period 1905-1910, in inspiration they belong to the nineteenth century, and at this juncture it may be well to mention Dali's growing devotion to certain aspects of that century's Romantic tradition. While French Romanticism seems to have impressed him little, except for such untypical manifestations as Lautréamont's *Chants de Maldoror* and the Louvre's Delacroix, *Still life with lobsters,* he has been more and more attracted to German Romanticism. One of his paintings of the Rosas period bears the revelatory title, *Instantaneous presence of Ludwig II of Bavaria, Salvador Dali, Lenin and Wagner on the beach at Rosas.* If the name of Lenin was included out of deference to Surrealism's Communist platform, that of Wagner was included for abidingly personal reasons. For Wagner was, and remains, the painter's favorite composer by far. The music for Dali's ballet, *Bacchanale* (1939), is of course from the Venusberg scene in *Tannhäuser.* A second ballet, *Mad Tristan* (1944), is based upon music from *Tristan und Isolde,* and there is no reason to doubt that Dali will some day suggest costumes, décor and choreographic action to accompany other Wagnerian music. The life of Wagner's mad patron, Ludwig II of Bavaria, has enthralled the painter, furnishing the central theme for his ballet, *Bacchanale,* as well as several episodes utilized in his art. Like de Chirico before him, Dali has also been absorbed in Nietzsche's thunderous message, and again following de Chirico's lead, he has acclaimed Arnold Böcklin as one of the master artists of all time. On his first visit to America in 1934, he was so moved by the Metropolitan Museum's Böcklin, *Isle of the Dead,* that he returned home to paint *Interior court of the 'Isle of the Dead'* and *Fountain of Böcklin.*

As a natural complement to the widening cultural allusion in Dali's art, the painter has come gradually to admire past artists in whom he had previously shown little interest. Although he continues to hail Meissonier as a great master, perhaps he has recently done so for the shock value which such a profession of respect cannot fail to have upon a generation trained to regard Meissonier as the epitome of the false-artistic. The painters whose art he has more seriously venerated of late are of a different order. Chief among them are Velasquez and Vermeer of Delft (an early enthusiasm as already noted), whom he has described as "the great Realist painters" (bibl. 56). The hard, broad modeling of Velasquez' early period, spent under the influence of Caravaggio, has been used by Dali in many works, of which *Impression of Africa* (page 64) and *Philosophy illuminated by the light of the moon and the setting sun* (page 71) are the most conspicuous examples. The influence of Velasquez'

16

later paintings on Dali is no less marked. It accounts in good part for the greater textural brilliance of more recent canvases by comparison with earlier paintings. In *Cardinal, cardinal!* (page 54), for example, the foreground figures, whose featureless heads resemble those of de Chirico's mannequins of 1915, are painted with a glittering impasto which seems specifically related to Velasquez' late technique. And if in recent works Dali has continued to employ the bland finish of "handmade photography," in a number of them he has used it as a foil to passages of radiant and thick texture. *Apparition of face and fruit-dish on a beach* (page 69) typifies his new, contrapuntal manipulation of pigment. Its broad glossy areas are broken at intervals by a richness of surface and tone which harks back to Velasquez' opulent handling of Spanish costume.

Dali's respect for the art of Jan Vermeer can only be described as obsessive. He has painted Vermeer's ghost (page 53); he has utilized the Rijksmuseum's *Young girl reading* as the basic theme of his own *The image disappears,* in which Vermeer's young girl is metamorphosed into a man with a beard; he has made Vermeer's "trade mark," the pearl, a symbol of cancerous beauty which that martyr-artist, the oyster, creates out of the slow irritation which may cause its death. At various times in his career he has declared that his ultimate ambition is to be able to paint like Vermeer, and having learned that an aged woman in Vienna had after forty years mastered the art of perfectly imitating Vermeer's technique, he prepared to visit her, only to learn that she had been driven away by Hitler's invading armies. His debt to Vermeer is not only avowed but apparent. It accounts for the yellow, pink and blue tonality of certain sections in his more recent paintings and for the quality of precision with which such a picture as *Two pieces of bread expressing the sentiment of love* (page 73) is handled.

Both *The ghost of Vermeer of Delft, which can be used as a table* (page 53) and *The weaning of furniture-nutrition* (page 54) illustrate a fundamental facet of Dali's "paranoia": his belief that the animate and the inanimate are interdependent in significance and function, with the inanimate taking its vitality from its relation to the living or from a strange capacity to come alive. Thus the leg of Vermeer's ghost serves as a table, while the chest of drawers in *The weaning of furniture-nutrition* owes its existence to the human nurse from whose back it has come and from whom it has itself derived the power to give birth to an infant chest of drawers. The most plausible basis for Dali's strange treatment of inanimate objects lies in his very obvious loathing of all mechanical things and forms, a loathing he expressed in his *Declaration of the Independence of the Imagination and the Rights of Man to His Own Madness,* wherein he advised his fellow-artists: "Only the violence and duration of your hardened dream can resist the hideous mechanical civilization that is your enemy . . ." An anti-mechanist in general philosophy, he has also been anti-mechanical in esthetics. The absolute opposite of an artist like Léger, who has drawn inspiration from contemporary machinery, Dali has consistently urged painters to turn their backs on the lifeless externals of modern civilization. "The history of the true creative artist," he has written, "is filled with the abuses and encroachments by means of which an absolute tyranny is imposed by the industrial mind over the new creative ideas of the poetic mind" (bibl. 61).

17

As already briefly noted, Dali's dislike for industrialism and its products may have been inherited from the artists of the *scuola metafisica* by whom he was influenced in youth. Yet his own reaction has been far more excessive than theirs. The signs of his contempt for the inanimate and the mechanical are many and characteristically extravagant. He has carried this contempt to the point of surrounding himself with furniture converted to living shapes: a sofa made to resemble Mae West's lips; a telephone concealed within a plaster lobster, "cold, green and aphrodisiac as the augur-troubled sleep of the cantharides" (bibl. 61). As part of his attempt to animate the lifeless, he has designed necklaces and bracelets which rotate slowly on their wearer's neck or arm, bringing into view a series of scabrous images. In the paintings *Palladio's corridor of Thalia* (page 63) and *Palladio's corridor of dramatic surprise* (page 67), he has changed to human form the stage properties through which Palladio achieved the astonishing foreshortening of his setting for the *Teatro Olimpico* in Vicenza. Wherever possible Dali has made living organism usurp, jeopardize or obviate the function of machinery and machine products; whenever possible, he has forced the inanimate to take part in action for which the essential requisite is animation itself. The tendency is further illustrated by such a painting as *Debris of an automobile giving birth to a blind horse biting a telephone* (page 66). The automobile is here given the ability to reproduce not itself but the horse, which in contemporary civilization it has nearly driven out of existence, but which now seems to emerge triumphant from the wreck of industrialism. The horse releases its fury by biting a telephone, a mechanical instrument which Dali considers so disastrous in connotation that at the time of the Munich Conference, arranged by telephone, he made the instrument the iconographical center of several paintings, among them *Imperial violets* and *The sublime moment* (page 65).

As far back as 1929 Dali had begun work on *The invisible man* (page 36), a major work in his career which was not completed until 1933. The picture furnishes proof, reinforced by his writings, that from the very beginning of his connection with Surrealism he has been fascinated by a visual phenomenon which has played an important part in the iconography of his paintings. This phenomenon is the double image—that is, the image which suggests or turns into a second image either at first glance or on being stared at intently. The phenomenon has been experienced by artists and laymen through the centuries. In painting, it was elaborately exploited by fantasists of the sixteenth and seventeenth centuries, among them Arcimboldo and Bracelli, by whom Dali claims his own interest in the phenomenon to have been directly inspired. For the Romantics of the nineteenth century, the double image held a special fascination. Early in the century, Delacroix made drawings of a lion's paw which turned into a human hand; at the century's end, Odilon Redon wrote in *A soi-même:* "The sense of mystery is always to be found in the equivocal, in double and triple aspects, suspicions of aspects (images within images), and in forms which are beginning to be or will begin to be, according to the state of mind of the observer." Popular artists, among them our own Currier and Ives, utilized the phenomenon in making picture puzzles, concealing almost endless images within the pattern of given subject matter. But Dali has gone further than any of his predecessors. He has not adopted the double image

The caprices and ingenious tricks of Mannerist artists and ornament designers of the period 1550-1650 were adapted by Dali for more serious purposes.

Arcimboldo, a master of double or composite images like the *Landscape-head* on page 20 (turn the page to see the head) may have influenced Dali in such works as those reproduced on pages 36, 69, and 74.

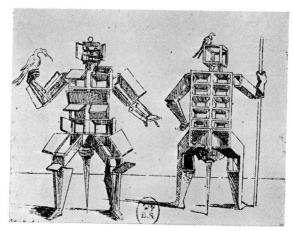

Above: the "furniture-figures" invented by Bracelli, another Mannerist artist, in his series of *Capricci* or *Bizarie* of 1624, influenced Dali directly in his *Weaning of furniture-nutrition* (page 54) and *Figure of drawers* (page 87).

Left: The ribbon figure at the left of Dali's *The triumph of Nautilus* (page 75) seems derived from Bracelli's ribbon figures. (See bibl. 188: items 5, 6, 53, 320, 323.)

as a *jeu d'esprit,* as the fantasists and popular artists did, nor has he been content to share the Romantics' conception of it as merely mysterious. Instead, he has proclaimed that the second, hallucinatory image suggested by a given object may be reality itself. In discussing multiple images in *La femme visible* he wrote: "I challenge materialists . . . to inquire into the more complex problem as to which of these images has the highest probability of existence if the intervention of desire is taken into account."

Dali believes that paranoiacs have a special capacity for the recognition of double images inasmuch as their disordered minds are hypersensitive to hidden appearances, real or imagined. That his own capacity for their recognition is extraordinary, no one can in fairness deny. On numerous occasions he has proved it beyond doubt, as when he discovered that the head in one of Picasso's paintings, on being turned sideways, almost exactly paralleled the image of an African village on a postcard in his own possession. (He painted a picture combining the images, entitled *The paranoiac face.*) He early defined the double image in terms of its reproduction in art as "such a representation of an object that it is also, without the slightest physical or anatomical change, the representation of another entirely different object, the second representation being equally devoid of any deformation

Arcimboldo, Tradition of: *Landscape—head* (double image). Late sixteenth century.

or abnormality betraying arrangement" (bibl. 52). In *The invisible man* and *Invisible sleeping woman, horse, lion* of 1930, he showed great ingenuity and imaginative skill in depicting double images in accordance with this definition, in both cases recording a dual identity which has a definite basis in abnormal psychology—a woman turning into a horse or lion.

In earlier paintings such as these, Dali was content to present two, or at most three, images in one. In the text of *La femme visible,* however, he made clear that he considered this numerical limitation arbitrary. "The double image," he wrote, ". . . may be extended, continuing the paranoiac advance, and then the presence of another dominant idea is enough to make a third image appear . . . and so on, until there is a number of images limited only by the mind's degree of paranoiac capacity." As his technique became more flexible, he consequently extended the sequence of images-within-images until in paintings such as *Apparition of face and fruit-dish on a beach* (page 69) he arrived at an astonishingly intricate succession of appearances and counter-appearances. By contrast with the Cubists, who had reduced the subject in painting to a minor and sometimes non-existent status, Dali provided his pictures with a sequence of subjects, each of them equally important and all of them interdependent. He reached a climax of complexity with *The endless enigma* of 1939, a canvas in which no less than six large-scale images are contained within the same over-all composition. Since that time the painter has returned to a simpler handling of the phenomenon of multiple images, as in such canvases as *Old age, adolescence, infancy* (page 74). Perhaps his most brilliant application of multiple images is to be found in *Spain* (frontispiece), surely a picture destined for a place in the history of the art of today.

The face of the central figure in *Spain* is defined by episodes from a cavalry combat after Leonardo, and it should here be mentioned that the Renaissance master belongs to the incongruous company of heroes celebrated in Dali's "paranoiac-critical" approach to esthetics. The reasons for his inclusion are evident. As already noted, Leonardo's iconography had been the subject of analysis by Dali's mentor, Sigmund Freud. Then the painter himself noted that "Leonardo proved an authentic innovator of paranoiac painting by recommending to his pupils that, for inspiration, in a certain frame of mind they regard the indefinite shapes of the spots of dampness and the cracks on the wall, that they might see immediately rise into view, out of the confused and the amorphous, the precise contours of the visceral tumult of an imaginary equestrian battle" (bibl. 171). Hence the cavalry combat used in *Spain* has become what the figures from Millet's *Angelus* were in earlier Dali paintings: a symbolic reference to an ideology which the artist finds related and sympathetic to his own. The combat has provided the theme of numerous drawings (pages 84 and 85). Dali's recent works also testify that his admiration for Leonardo has not been merely ideological. The enigmatic face of da Vinci's Madonnas is utilized for the foreground figure in *Inventions of the monsters* (page 62) and recurs in other canvases, while Leonardo's technical influence on Dali's craftsmanship is in certain cases unmistakable.

Simultaneously with his development of the multiple image, Dali has adapted to his own use a related visual phenomenon: that of the object which, once seen, recurs in the imagination time and again, sometimes varying as to identity and scale but always remaining the same in general outline. For want of a better term, the phenomenon may be called that of the repetitive form. It has been more or less widely experienced, since nearly everyone has at times been troubled by a shape which recurs everywhere, assuming inexplicable guise. Its previous usage in art covers a long chronological span: in the 15th century Mérode altarpiece by the Flemish Master of Flémalle, Joseph's mousetrap is close in form to the village well seen through the open window of his shop; in 1924 Max Ernst explored the device's possibilities in *Two children are menaced by a nightingale,* a picture whose influence on Dali has been suggested by a critic (bibl. 158). Dali has recorded his own "paranoiac" sensitivity to the phenomenon in a number of paintings. Thus in *The weaning of furniture-nutrition* the chest of drawers leaves its own outline in the nurse's back and in turn gives birth to a smaller chest identical in shape. In *Nostalgic echo* (page 57) the bell in the tower becomes in succession a girl skipping rope, a keyhole in the chest of drawers, and a shadowy figure standing under the far arcade. As in the case of the multiple image, Dali believes the recognition of repetitive images to be limited only by "paranoiac" capacity.

In the years immediately prior to the outbreak of the recent war Dali made three extended visits to Italy. The effect of these visits has been increasingly evident in his painting. Not only has close familiarity with the great Italian tradition still further moderated his disdain for established esthetic standards, but the impact of this tradition has altered and widened his own technical means. To his list of preferred painters of the past must now be added a new galaxy: Botticelli, whose *Birth of Venus* was later to be emblazoned across the façade of Dali's Dream House at the World's Fair in New York; Piero di Cosimo, who in Dali's words "observed the viscous and mucous and bloody contours of tuberculer [sic] spit, that there might rise into view enigmatic and atavistic compositions, fire and the horrible dragon of the oyster" (bibl. 171); Raphael, whose figures de Chirico had described as phantasmal and statuesque, and whose *St. George and the dragon* Dali considers the finest painting in America; and Uccello, long since hailed as a precursor of Surrealism by André Breton himself. Apart from these and other masters of the Renaissance, he has developed a new esteem for painters of Mannerism and the Baroque. Caravaggio has joined Vermeer and Velasquez in the inner circle of his idols, and both *Impression of Africa* and *Philosophy illuminated by the light of the moon and the setting sun,* however close to the early Velasquez in spirit, relate back to Caravaggio himself in their dramaturgy and in the bold handling of their foreshortening and chiaroscuro. *Debris of an automobile giving birth to a blind horse biting a telephone,* whatever its relation to a passage in Picasso's *Guernica,* has a definite affinity to the jeweled night scenes of the Baroque tradition.

The influence of the Baroque is particularly noticeable in *Palladio's corridor of Thalia, Palladio's corridor of dramatic surprise* and *Group of women imitating the gestures of a schooner* (page 72). The first two pictures are exuberantly handled, with obvious relish in values of impasto, and their long, slashing high lights suggest the technique of Magnasco. In the last-named canvas the background figure, constructed of circular brushstrokes, seems directly inspired by Bracelli's figures composed of typographers' scrolls, while the rushing tension between the foreground figures is prefigured in certain paintings of the Italian Baroque such as Guido Reni's famous *Atalanta and Hippomenes*. But if the frenzied motion of all three paintings relates them to the Baroque, their elegant elongation of forms derives from pre-Baroque Mannerism. It seems likely, however, that Dali's Mannerist distortions more often have been adapted from Spanish than from Italian sources; certainly they pre-date his absorption in sixteenth-century Italian art. Just as Picasso in youth had borrowed stylistic devices from Morales, El Greco and other Spanish artists of the Mannerist tradition, so Dali from the very beginning of his career has come under the influence of native Mannerism. This influence may be detected in the exaggerated muscularity and diminutive feet of the figures in the right background of *The old age of William Tell* (page 41), and it recurs at intervals throughout his work. In certain of his most recent paintings the dominant style is that of Mannerism turned "psychological," in the contemporary sense of the latter term.

Dali's devotion to the Italian tradition has brought him into closer relationship to the Neo-Romantic artists, particularly Bérard, Berman and Tchelitchew, whose own inspiration has so often derived from Italian sources. The signs of this kinship have, however, been long developing. To the post-abstract vocabulary of Parisian painting, both the Surrealists and the Neo-Romantics have from the beginning contributed, and from it both groups have drawn freely. The vocabulary's terminology is Romantic, although it has largely escaped the cumbrance of literary conceit which finally reduced the nineteenth-century Romantic tradition to pedantry. Through it have been re-stated, among other things, the imaginative elegance and fantasy upon which the Cubists had turned their backs, following the lead of Cézanne, whom Dali was characteristically to dismiss as a "platonic mason" (bibl. 97). And if Dali has given the new vocabulary much of its vigor and been accountable for its extravagance of phrase and use of *double entendre,* he has lately been impressed by the scholarly terms of the Neo-Romantics. In recent years he has deeply admired the works of Christian Bérard which, although few in number, have earned Bérard an important, if rather special, position in recent Parisian art. The head of the principal figure in Dali's *The triumph of Nautilus* (page 75) seems specifically based upon the heads in Bérard's wash drawings. The elegiac grace of the figures and the inclusion of architectural fragments in *Old age, adolescence, infancy* may be ascribed partially to the influence of Bérard and Berman. Yet it must immediately be said that Dali's impact upon the Neo-Romantics may be just as precisely measured. The truth of the matter is that in contributing mutually to a post-abstract vocabulary, Dali and the Neo-Romantics have tended to lessen the contradiction in their respective means of expression. Whereas Dali was once partially somnambulist in inspiration and the Neo-Romantics were by comparison naturalist, now all have progressed to a ground which becomes increasingly common to all. The difference between *Accommodations of desire* (page 35) and a typical Neo-Romantic painting of 1929 was almost irreconcilable. Between *Old age, adolescence, infancy* and certain Neo-Romantic works of today it is a difference of vision and temperament rather than a basic difference of kind.

With the *Family of marsupial centaurs* (page 76) the evolution of Dali's ideology appeared to have come full circle. For the painting summarized in extreme degree the artist's decision TO BECOME CLASSIC, as the foreword to his 1941 exhibition proclaimed in bold type, to paint pictures "uniquely consecrated to the architecture of the Renaissance and to the Special Sciences" (bibl. 172). As even the most casual observer will note, the painting's composition is rigidly based on intersecting diagonals which divide the picture space into four equilateral triangles. The disposition of forms is regulated with forethought and certainty, and not a single gesture or wayward line is allowed to break the pattern of triangles and parallels. Whereas a few years previously Dali had shown his contempt for the classic formulas of composition by balancing the heavy left section of *Inventions of the monsters* with an almost invisible blue dog in the right foreground, he now reverted to the most sacrosanct rules of symmetry. *Family of marsupial centaurs* was plainly in full reaction against his earlier works wherein composition was avowedly determined by subconscious inspiration and based on the asymmetric laws of accident.

The tendency exhibited in *Family of marsupial centaurs* was an indication that Dali's whole program was in need of drastic revision. The change in direction, though never again so dramatically apparent, did not come without warning. To anyone at all familiar with Surrealist activity during the period 1935-1941, it was clear that the bonds between Dali and the Surrealist movement were wearing thin. For while the Surrealists continued to concern themselves with revelations of subconscious thought and to repose their hopes on group effort, Dali year by year moved nearer a conscious objectivity, the focal point of which, perhaps inevitably, was himself. The Surrealists consequently rejected as impure and egocentric the obsessions which Dali recorded primarily because they proceeded from an intensely private megalomania in which he had great faith. It was Dali the solitary "madman" rather than Dali the Surrealist who wrote in 1941: "The two luckiest things that can happen to a contemporary painter are: first to be Spanish, and second to be named Dali. Both have happened to me" (bibl. 172). During the war, which disrupted Surrealism as a cohesive movement, Dali allowed his inspiration to rise nearer and nearer the surface of his mind, where dwells reason, the mortal enemy of the subconscious. Indeed, in 1942 and 1943 he relied for initial impetus on outer appearance in one of its most traditional pictorial forms—portraiture.

Whether Dali would have heeded the dictates of reason without having had the blessing of Surrealism's greatest hero, Sigmund Freud, is an intricate problem. But shortly before Freud's death Dali met him in London and heard him say: "What interests me in your art is not the unconscious but the conscious." Though this had been more and more what interested Dali himself, he may understandably have taken final courage from Freud's pronouncement. He may then and there have determined to paint a picture such as *Family of marsupial centaurs*. When he did so, for whatever reason, he inevitably reversed the whole Surrealist procedure and brought it back near its starting point. For whereas the Surrealists had eagerly brushed aside conscious thought in order to peer into the dark wells of the subconscious, Dali was now ready to scrutinize his subconscious for signs it might contain of conscious reason. When these signs appeared, as they so plainly did in *Family of marsupial centaurs*, he hailed them with much the same enthusiasm the Surrealists had shown when they first plumbed the subconscious and found images of astonishing beauty.

We know now, however, that during the five years which have elapsed since *Family of marsupial centaurs* was painted, Dali has never reverted to so classical a formula. While inveighing against "the complete sterility and fumbling of automatism built out of all proportion into an absolute system," he adds that Raphael "gave the exact proportion and degree of automatism desirable in a work of art when, after having affirmed, 'I paint according to a certain idea,' he advised that at the moment of execution one must always think of something else" (bibl. 162). Thus the symmetrical plan of *Resurrection of the flesh* (page 77) was presumably determined when the picture was begun "according to a certain idea" in 1940. But as completed in 1945, the composition is broken by fitful Mannerist motifs; some of the painter's earlier violence has returned, though in the more painterly guise announced by the Neo-Baroque *Philosophy illuminated by the light of the moon and the setting sun*. And while *Resurrection of the flesh* is in a sense an anthology of Dali's iconography of the late 1930s, *Uranium and atomica melancholica idyll* (page 81) reveals new symbolic preoccupations — baseball players, aeroplane faces, bombs shaped like the planets of Grandville and René Magritte, a split watch equipped with a tongue, the doughy, convoluted head which also appears in the *Apotheosis of Homer* (page 80).

If Dali is still shaken occasionally by the fantastic fevers of his youth, he has sometimes turned recently to the plainer realism which he used during the period 1925-1927 in alternation with more abstract styles. *The basket of bread* of 1945 (page 81) resolves with new brilliance of technique the objective problems posed by his picture of the same subject, painted almost twenty years before (page 30). *My wife, nude, contemplating her own flesh becoming stairs, three vertebrae of a column, sky and architecture* (page 79) is a restatement in deliberately more academic terms of the fantasy expressed in *The weaning of furniture-nutrition.*

Dali's interest in imaginative elegance continues unabated. His portraits of 1942 and 1943 were mostly of leading figures in the world of fashion; they rather unsuccessfully combined strict representational likeness with marginal allusions to previous, more inventive works. Fortunately his taste for Baroque extravaganza has been more impressively recorded elsewhere, notably in *The broken bridge and the dream* (page 78) and in fine recent drawings, such as *The fountains* (page 91), which convert Picasso's dotted calligraphy for Balzac's *Le Chef-d'oeuvre inconnu* into a personal vehicle for *capricci.*

Whatever the future's judgment of Dali may be, it cannot be based solely on his accomplishments as a painter. From the very beginning of his career, he has striven to revive the Renaissance ideal of the artist as a man whose talents are applicable to the whole problem of esthetics. He has, for instance, worked seriously and steadily as a writer. In doing so he has furnished one more indication of his reaction against the beliefs of the older modern artists. Among leaders of the first School of Paris generation, only Rouault and de Chirico have consistently practiced literature, while Matisse, Braque and, until recently, Picasso have strictly and purposefully confined their expression to the plastic arts. Dali, on the other hand, has already completed an impressive list of poems, prose pieces and articles (see bibl.). In contrast to his elders, who have done their best to isolate their art from literary influences, he has gone so far as to write a poem (bibl. 75) to be played on a phonograph as the observer looks at his painting, *Narcissus.* There is additional proof of his desire to explore fields which the older Parisian painters have considered alien to their profession. While Matisse constantly attends the moving pictures in order to forget completely his labors as an artist, Dali regards the cinema as a medium for which he, as a painter, is ideally suited. He has collaborated with Luis Bunuel on the scenarios and direction of two films, *Un Chien Andalou* (1929) and *L'Age d'Or* (1931); he has recently designed a nightmare sequence for the Hollywood film, *Spellbound,* directed by Alfred Hitchcock; he is now at work in the Disney Studios on a long animated cartoon.

Within the realm of the older visual arts, Dali has ranged wider than members of the Picasso generation though not wider than the 1890 generation of Symbolists. He has designed furniture and jewelry and collaborated with Schiaparelli and Chanel in creating fashions, all in addition to the tasks of mural decoration and theater design in which his elders have also at various times been absorbed. His widespread activity may be ascribed partially to his

25

connection with Surrealism, since that movement has discouraged the close devotion to métier in which Derain, for instance, has believed no less passionately than did Renoir. Following the lead of Marcel Duchamp, and to a lesser degree of Picasso, the Surrealists have attempted to show that art objects or anti-art objects may rival easel paintings in emotional force and validity, and Dali has consequently created innumerable articles from all manner of material, most of them reconstructions of dream imagery. They vary widely in size and intent, from an aphrodisiac smoking jacket to the famous raining taxi in which sat Columbus, whom Dali believes to have been a paranoiac, because in insisting that the world was round and hence endless, he betrayed a fear that he might be cornered by imaginary pursuers.

Since 1936 Dali's interest in the minor arts may have been further stimulated by his respect for the accomplishments of the Pre-Raphaelites. This interest has, of course, been shared by a few younger Surrealists and by the Neo-Romantics, among artists associated with art activity originally centered in Paris. But only Dali has been willing to claim for his work in minor media an importance equal to that of his painting. While the others have quite understandably wished to be judged first of all as painters and sculptors, Dali has at times defended his art objects as against his own canvases. Surely he alone could say in all seriousness, as he recently did, "Cellini was a much greater artist than Michelangelo."

This review of Dali's career to date has purposefully been restricted to a discussion of the painter's technical and ideological development. The question of his position in contemporary art is at least partially answered by the indubitable fact that he is the most famous of the younger artists and that his influence, whether negatively or positively, has been widely felt. Perhaps this question may not now be answered more exactly. Even now, however, it seems clear that Dali has brought to a head the particular kind of anti-abstract revolt which had begun five years before his arrival in Paris among younger Parisian artists taking their direction from the early period of Giorgio de Chirico. In America as well he has helped restore representational painting in general, and objective exactitude of technique in particular, to a popular favor which they might have rewon more slowly without him. The success of the reaction against abstract art for which he stands has not been complete in that the abstract movement continues to thrive, nourished on Picasso's boundless energy, Mondrian's dogma and Miro's inventiveness. But the reaction has at least succeeded in establishing itself securely in contemporary esthetics.

There is a problem related solely to Dali's emergence as a public figure which deserves some comment. Is he an isolated phenomenon projected into fame by an unusual technique, a weird imagination and a flair for publicity? Or does he reflect, in exaggerated form, the psychology of his epoch? Is he pure eccentric or part prophet? Although parallels between an artist and his time are frequently of dubious validity when drawn by a contemporary, there are a few in Dali's case which at least carry the weight of plausible conjecture.

To begin with, even the most determined Narcissus cannot isolate his own image, and the pool into which Dali has stared so fixedly carries reflections of his surroundings that no flurry of pebbles can dispel. His former identification with Surrealism, which to many once

26

signified a childish retreat from reality, may now conceivably be re-read as a passionate espousal of a counter-reality to which all France, all civilized Europe, had been clinging for assurance. The double image no longer appears so personal a device in a world where statesmen as well as painters have portrayed objectives with such cunning that they have become "without the slightest physical or anatomical change, the representation of another entirely different object, the second representation being equally devoid of any deformation or abnormality betraying arrangement." In view of the frightful havoc which machines have lately wrought on earth, one may properly inquire whether Dali's loathing of them has been merely egocentric and exhibitionistic. To narrow the question, one may ask which type of architecture more accurately diagnosed the hidden psychosis of the years just before the war: *machines à habiter,* with their flat white roofing and broad areas of glass; or the small, dark, womblike houses which Dali proposed to build as retreats from a mechanical civilization and which, as air raid shelters, recently covered the landscape of England.

That the era in which Dali has come to fame has been one of immense neuroticism, few will any longer deny. It has been an era of stepped-up emotion, of restlessness and phobias to which artists, having figuratively one less layer of skin than laymen, have naturally been sensitive. The anatomy of the era has been an anatomy of nerves, its spiritual regeneration reduced to therapeutic measures. In America, where Dali's fame has been the greatest, large sections of the public have acquired a taste for vicariously experiencing all manner of violent sensations. The tabloids, radio and moving pictures have fed the taste with a cunning hand, and in vast numbers of people a ferocious appetite for the morbid has been induced which only the horror of war has perhaps brought at last to prime satiety. The question inevitably arises: in paying heed to Dali, has the epoch been paying heed to itself?

To suggest the maximum significance of Dali's hold on popular consciousness is not to preclude the chance that this significance may be less deeply rooted than certain parallels indicate. The matter of intrinsic worth aside, fame has often come to artists for reasons which history has gone halt pursuing. It may be that Dali is an isolated phenomenon, for whom Freud's epithet, "What a fanatic!" is apt and final, as Dali has proudly proclaimed it. If this be true, then to Dali must be said what Victor Hugo respectfully wrote to no less a poet than Charles Baudelaire: "You create a new shudder."

JAMES THRALL SOBY

BRIEF CHRONOLOGY

1904 Born in Figueras, Spain.

c.1918 Admired 19th century Spanish painters of genre scenes, the French and Spanish Impressionists.

c.1920 Influenced by Italian Futurism which led him to cubism.

1921 Went to Madrid to study the paintings in the Prado; enrolled in the *Escuela Especial de Pintura, Escultura y Grabado* (Madrid School of Fine Arts).

1923–1925 Painted under the influence of the "Metaphysical School" of Italian artists (1915-1919), notably Giorgio de Chirico and Carlo Carrà.

1924 Suspended from the Madrid School of Fine Arts for a year; imprisoned in Figueras and Gerona for political activity.

1925–1926 Began to exhibit in Madrid and Barcelona, achieving considerable local fame as a leading Catalan painter of the young generation.
Permanently expelled from the Madrid School of Fine Arts, 1926.

1925–1927 Painted in several distinct and conflicting styles: realism (under the influence of the Dutch 17th century artists, especially Vermeer); cubism (influenced by Picasso and Gris); abstraction (influenced by Picasso's 1924 still lifes); Neo-Classicism (influenced by Picasso's Neo-Classic figure style of the early 1920s).

1927 Completed *Blood is sweeter than honey* and other works which announce the fantastic art of subconscious obsessions by which he has become widely known.

1928 Visited Paris; met the Surrealist writers and painters.

1929 Decided definitely to devote his art to the literal transcription of his dreams and "paranoiac" visions (summer).
Moved to Paris and became an official Surrealist (fall).
First Paris exhibition, Galerie Goemans.
Collaborated with Luis Bunuel on a short film, *Un Chien Andalou*.

1929–1931 Influenced by early period of de Chirico, by Max Ernst, Yves Tanguy and *art nouveau* decoration and furniture.
Inspired by Arcimboldo and Bracelli, began painting double images in *The invisible man*.

1930 Published *La Femme Visible*, giving his theories of "paranoiac" inspiration. Called his technique "handmade photography," related it to that of Meissonier.

1930–1934 Paintings reflected his obsession with a Freudian conception of the legend of William Tell and, slightly later, of *The Angelus* of Millet.

1931 Collaborated with Luis Bunuel on a full-length film, *L'Age d'Or*.

1933 First New York one-man show, Julien Levy Gallery.

1933–1934 "Bone" series; figures with cephalic deformations.

1934 Illustrated Lautréamont's *Les Chants de Maldoror*.
First visit to U. S. A. Nov. 14.

1934–1936 Beach scenes at Rosas (Spain), with "instantaneous" figures.

1936 Decorations (murals) for the residence of Edward James, London.

1937–1939 Increasingly admired Vermeer and Velasquez.
Three visits to Italy brought him new appreciation of Renaissance and Baroque painting and architecture.

1939 Designed and supervised construction of Dali's Dream of Venus, erected in amusement area of the World's Fair, New York.
Wrote book, designed costumes and décor for the ballet, *Bacchanale*.

1940 Returned to the United States August 16. Has resided here ever since, mainly at Del Monte, California.

1941 Wrote book, designed costumes and décor for the ballet, *Labyrinth*. Large retrospective exhibition, The Museum of Modern Art, New York.

1942 Published his autobiography, *The Secret Life of Salvador Dali*.

1942–1943 Executed a series of portraits, exhibited at the Knoedler Galleries, N. Y. (1943). Completed mural decorations for the home of Princess Artchil Gourielli, N. Y.

1944 Published a novel, *Hidden Faces*.
Wrote the book and designed the costumes and décor for two ballets, *Sentimental Colloquy* and *Mad Tristan*.
Painted a series of panels depicting the seven arts for lobby display in Billy Rose's production of *The Seven Lively Arts*.
Illustrated Maurice Sandoz' *Fantastic Memories*.

1945 Exhibition of recent paintings and drawings, Bignou Gallery, New York.
Illustrated Maurice Sandoz' *The Maze*.

Still life. 1924. Oil on canvas. Private collection.

Harlequin. Ca. 1925. Oil on canvas, ca. 8 x 6 feet.
Collection of the artist.

Girl sewing. 1926. Oil on panel?

The basket of bread. 1926. Oil on panel, 14 x 13¾ inches. Private collection.

Still life. 1926. Oil on canvas.

Neo-Cubist Academy. 1926. Oil on canvas.

Figures on the sand. 1926-27. Oil on canvas.

Blood is sweeter than honey. 1927. Oil on canvas.

Apparatus and hand. 1927. Oil on canvas.

Illumined pleasures. 1929. Oil on panel, 9⅜ x 13⅝ inches. Collection Sidney Janis.

Accommodations of desire. 1929. Oil on panel, 8⅝ x 13¾ inches. Collection Wright Ludington.

The invisible man. 1929-33 (incomplete state). Oil on canvas. Collection the Vicomte de Noailles.

The font. 1930. Oil on composition board, 26 x 16¼ inches. Collection Mr. and Mrs. A. Reynolds Morse.

The feeling of becoming. 1930. Oil on canvas, 13¾ x 10⅝ inches. Collection Mrs. W. Murray Crane.

38

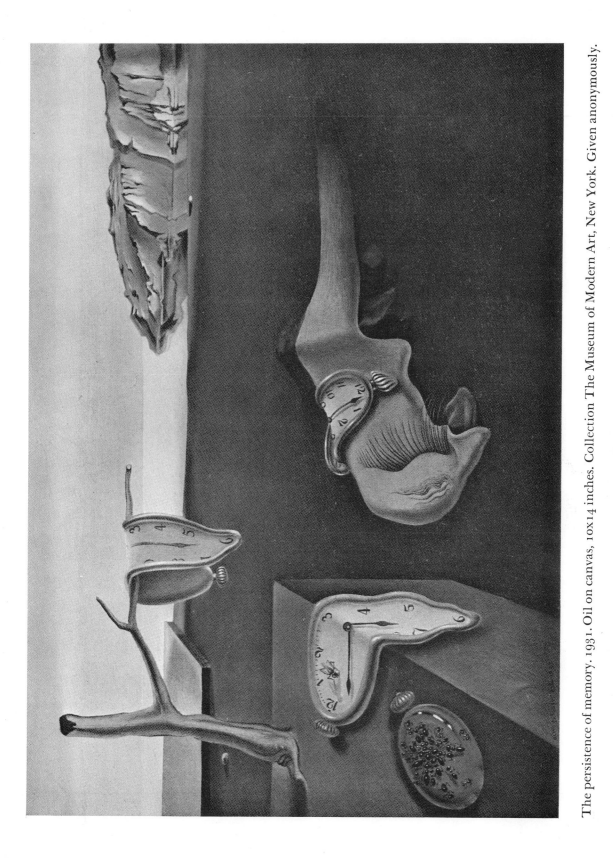

The persistence of memory. 1931. Oil on canvas, 10x14 inches. Collection The Museum of Modern Art, New York. Given anonymously.

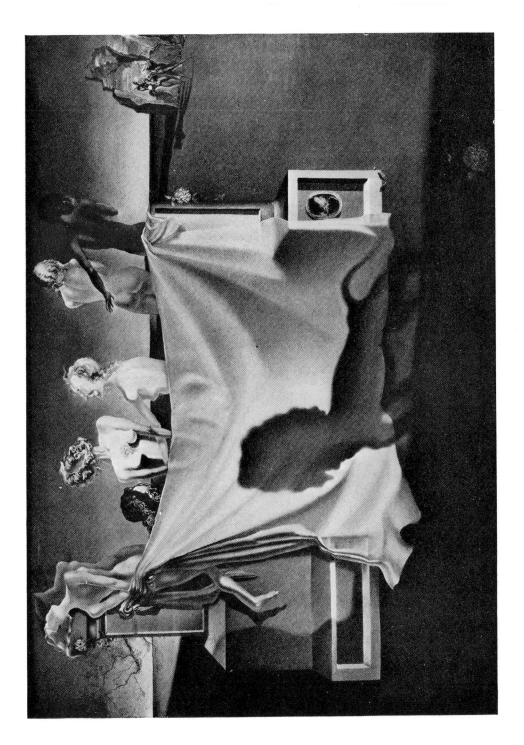

The old age of William Tell. 1931. Oil on canvas. Collection the Vicomte de Noailles.

Shades of night descending. 1931. Oil on canvas, 24 x 19¾ inches. Collection Mr. and Mrs. A. Reynolds Morse.

Agnostic symbol. 1932. Oil on canvas, 26¾ x 25¼ inches. The University of California at Los Angeles. Walter C. Arensberg Collection.

Myself at the age of ten when I was the grasshopper child. 1933. Oil on panel, 8⅞ x 6¾ inches. Collection Dr. Charles E. Roseman, Jr.

The phantom cart. 1933. Oil on panel, 6 x 8½ inches. Collection Thomas Fine Howard.

Gala and the Angelus of Millet immediately preceding the arrival of the conic anamorphoses. 1933. Oil on panel, 9⅜ x 7⅜ inches. Collection Henry P. McIlhenny.

Javanese mannequin. 1933-34. Oil on canvas, 25 x 21 inches. Collection Dr. Charles E. Roseman, Jr.

The spectre of sex appeal. 1934. Oil on panel, 7 x 5½ inches. Collection of the artist.

Average atmospherocephalic bureaucrat in the act of milking a cranial harp. 1933. Oil on canvas, 8¾ x 6½ inches. Collection Mr. and Mrs. A. Reynolds Morse.

Aerodynamic chair. 1934. Oil on panel, 8⅝ x 6¼ inches. Collection De Beers Consolidated Mines, Ltd.

50

Symbol of anguish. 1934. Oil on panel, 8¾ x 6⅜ inches. Collection Mrs. Irving T. Snyder.

Enigmatic elements in a landscape. 1934. Oil on panel, 28⅝ x 23½ inches. Collection The International Business Machines Corp.

The ghost of Vermeer of Delft, which can be used as a table. 1934. Oil on panel, 7⅛ x 5½ inches. Private collection.

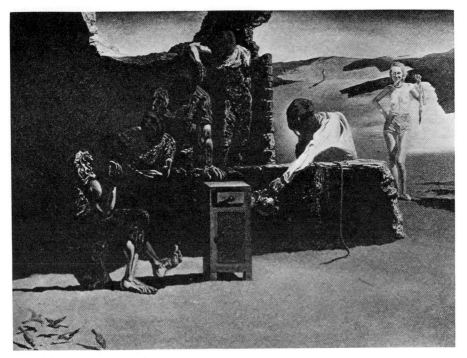

Cardinal, cardinal! 1934. Oil on panel, 6⅜ x 8⅝ inches. Collection Arthur Bradley Campbell.

The weaning of furniture-nutrition. 1934. Oil on canvas. Private collection.

Paranoiac-astral image. 1934. Oil on panel, 6¼ x 8⅝ inches. The Wadsworth Atheneum, Hartford.

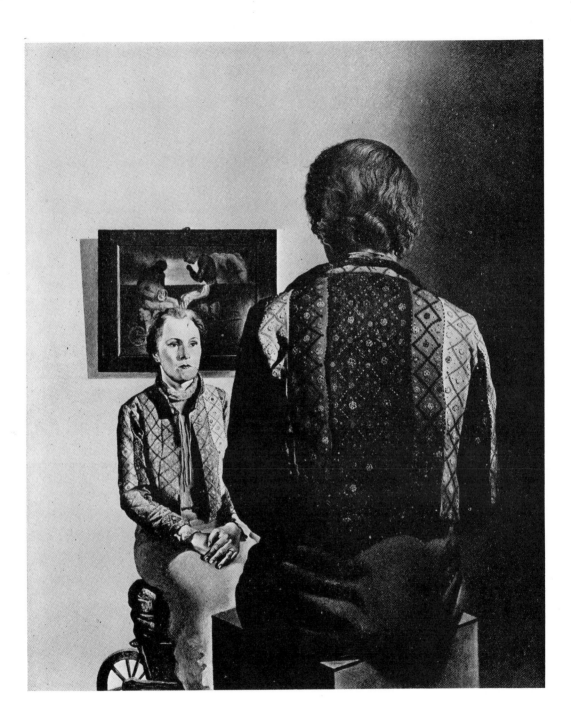

Portrait of Gala. 1935. Oil on panel, 12¾ x 10½ inches. The Museum of Modern Art, New York. Given anonymously.

56

Nostalgic echo. 1935. Oil on canvas, 38¼ x 38¼ inches. Collection Dr. and Mrs. Leslie M. Maitland.

Noon. 1936. Oil on canvas, 35⅜ x 45½ inches. Private collection.

A chemist lifting with extreme precaution the cuticle of a grand piano. 1936. Oil on canvas, 19¾ x 25½ inches. Collection Miss Ruth Page.

The man with the head of blue hortensias. 1936. Oil on canvas, 6⅜ x 8⅝ inches. Private collection.

Three young surrealist women holding in their arms the skins of an orchestra. 1936. Oil on canvas, 21¼ x 25⅝ inches. Collection Thomas A. Fransioli, Jr.

Soft construction with boiled beans; premonition of civil war. 1936. Oil on canvas, 39½ x 33 inches. The University of California at Los Angeles. Walter C. Arensberg Collection.

Inventions of the monsters. 1937. Oil on canvas, 20⅛ x 30⅞ inches. The Art Institute of Chicago. The Joseph Winterbotham Collection.

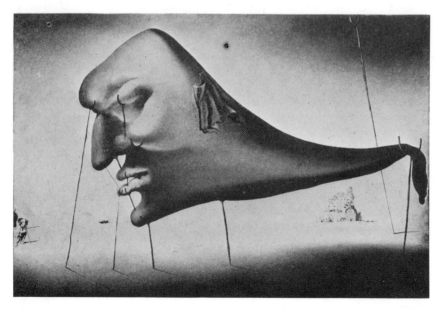

Sleep. 1937. Oil on canvas, 20 x 30¾ inches. Collection Edward James.

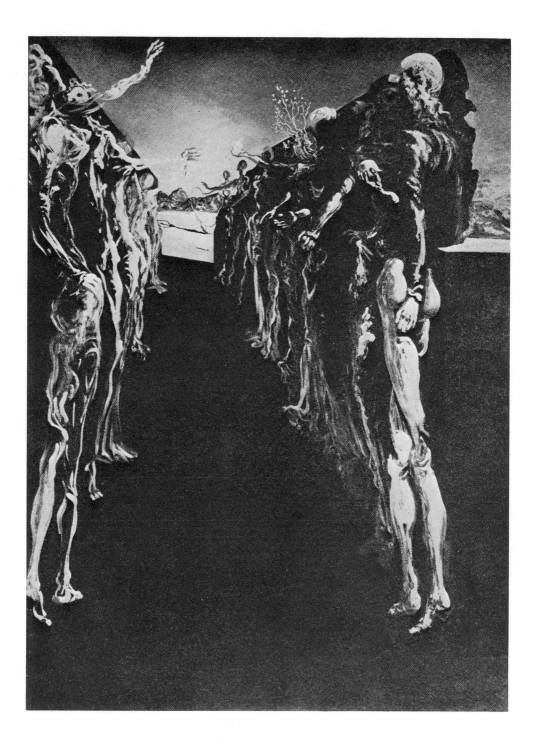

Palladio's corridor of Thalia. 1937. Oil on canvas, 46¼ x 35⅝ inches. Collection
Edward James.

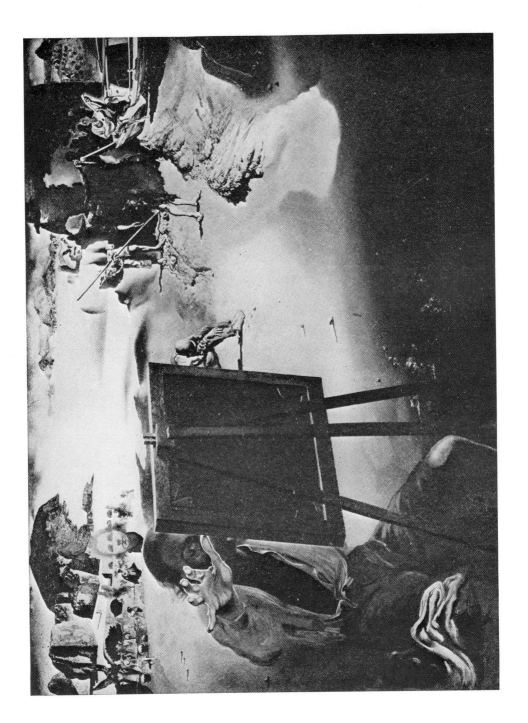

Impression of Africa. 1938. Oil on canvas, 36 x 46¼ inches. Collection Edward James.

The sublime moment. 1938. Oil on canvas, 15½ x 18½ inches.
Collection Dr. and Mrs. Theodore W. Braasch.

Imperial violets. 1938. Oil on canvas, 39¼ x 56⅛ inches. The Museum of
Modern Art, New York. Gift of Edward James.

Debris of an automobile giving birth to a blind horse biting a telephone. 1938. Oil on canvas, 21¼ x 25½ inches. Private collection.

Palladio's corridor of dramatic surprise. 1938. Oil on canvas, 28¾ x 41 inches. Private collection, New York.

Apparition of face and fruit-dish on a beach. 1938. Oil on canvas, 45 x 57½ inches. The Wadsworth Atheneum, Hartford.

Psychoanalysis and morphology meet. 1939. Oil on canvas, 10 x 18⅜ inches. Collection
Mrs. Gerard B. Lambert.

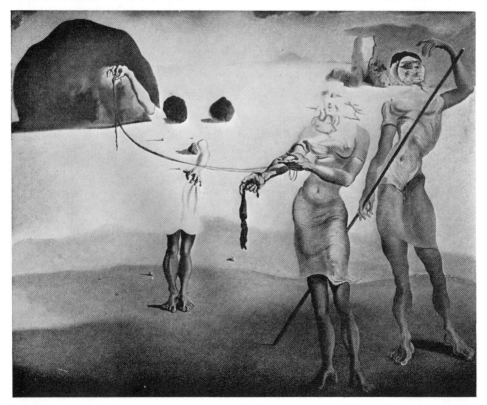

Enchanted beach with three fluid graces. 1938-39. Oil on canvas, 25½ x 31½
inches. Collection Dr. Charles E. Roseman, Jr.

Philosophy illuminated by the light of the moon and the setting sun. 1939. Oil on canvas, 51 x 64 inches. Collection Alfonso Gonzalez.

Group of women imitating the gestures of a schooner. 1940. Oil on canvas, 21½ x 25¾ inches. Collection Mrs. Harold McCormick.

Two pieces of bread expressing the sentiment of love. 1940. Oil on canvas, 32¼ x 39½ inches. Collection of the artist.

Two pieces of bread expressing the sentiment of love *(detail)*.

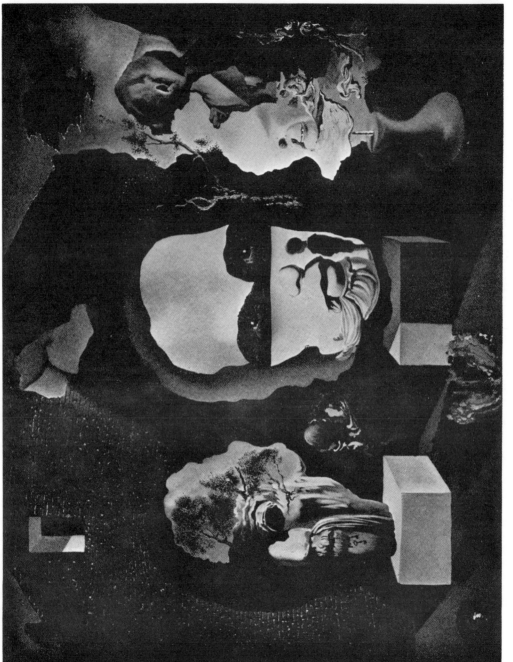

Old age, adolescence, infancy. 1940. Oil on canvas, 19⅝ x 25⅝ inches. Collection Alfonso Gonzalez.

74

The triumph of Nautilus. 1941. Oil on canvas, 11⅛ x 13⅞ inches. Collection Miss Vera Zorina.

Family of marsupial centaurs. 1941. Oil on canvas. Collection Alfonso Gonzalez.

76

Resurrection of the flesh. 1940-45. Oil on canvas, 36 x 29 inches. Collection John Perona.

The broken bridge and the dream. 1945. Oil on canvas, 26 x 34 inches. Collection Dr. Charles E. Roseman, Jr.

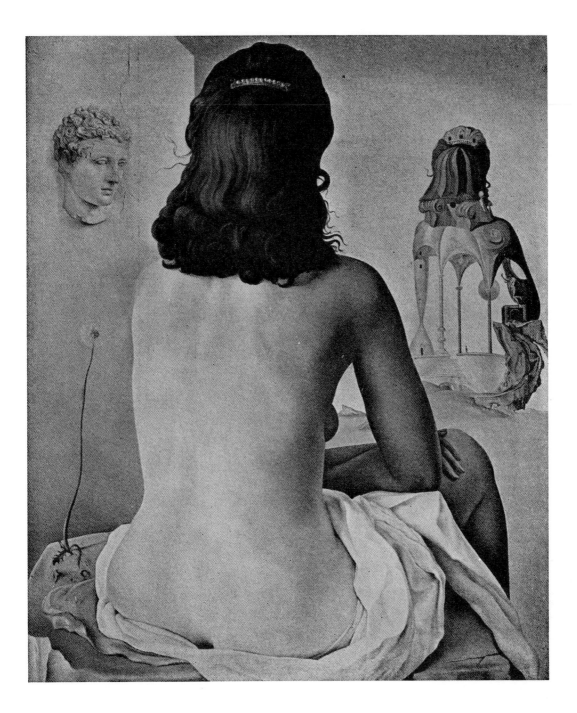

My wife, nude, contemplating her own flesh becoming stairs, three vertebrae of a column, sky and architecture. 1945. Oil on panel, 24 x 20 inches. Collection John Perona.

Apotheosis of Homer (Diurnal dream of Gala). 1944-45. Oil on canvas, 25 x 46 inches. Collection Alfonso Gonzalez.

Uranium and atomica melancholica idyll. 1945. Oil on canvas, 26 x 34 inches.
Bignou Gallery, New York.

The basket of bread. 1945. Oil on panel, 13 x 15 inches.
Collection of the artist.

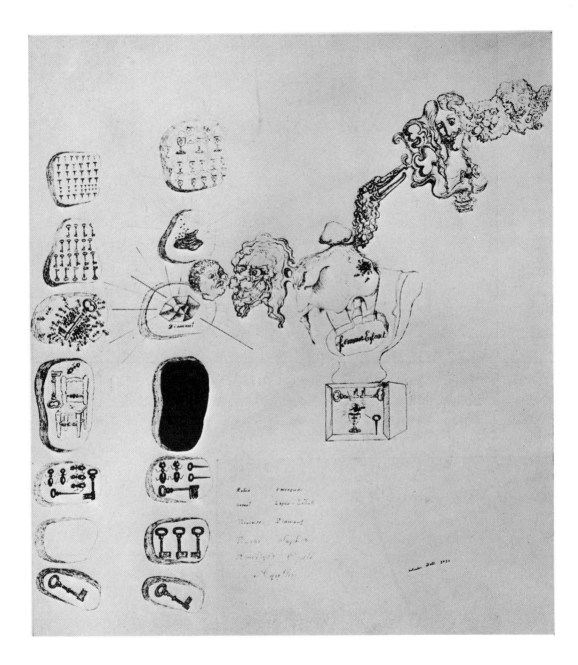

Frontispiece for the second surrealist manifesto. 1930. Ink and watercolor, 12 x 10¾ inches. Collection Sidney Janis.

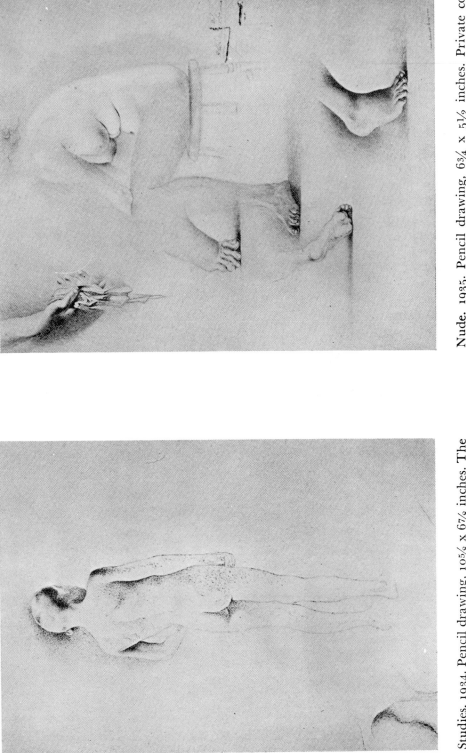

Nude. 1935. Pencil drawing, 6¾ x 5½ inches. Private collection.

Studies. 1934. Pencil drawing, 10⅝ x 6⅞ inches. The Wadsworth Atheneum, Hartford.

83

Anthropomorphic echo. 1936. Ink and pencil, 20½ x 17 inches. Collection Mrs. Rip C. Underwood.

Study of horsemen. 1936. Ink drawing, 17 x 21 inches. The Museum of Modern Art, New York. Gift of Sam A. Lewisohn.

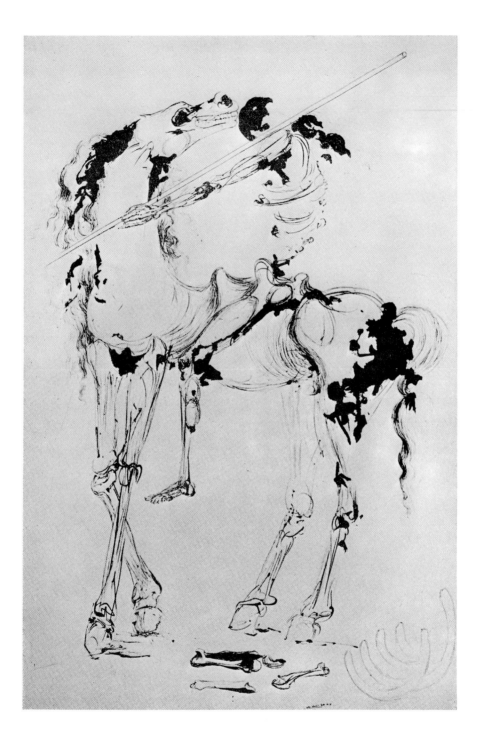

Cavalier of death. 1936. Ink drawing, 33½ x 22⅜ inches. Collection Mrs.
Stanley Resor.

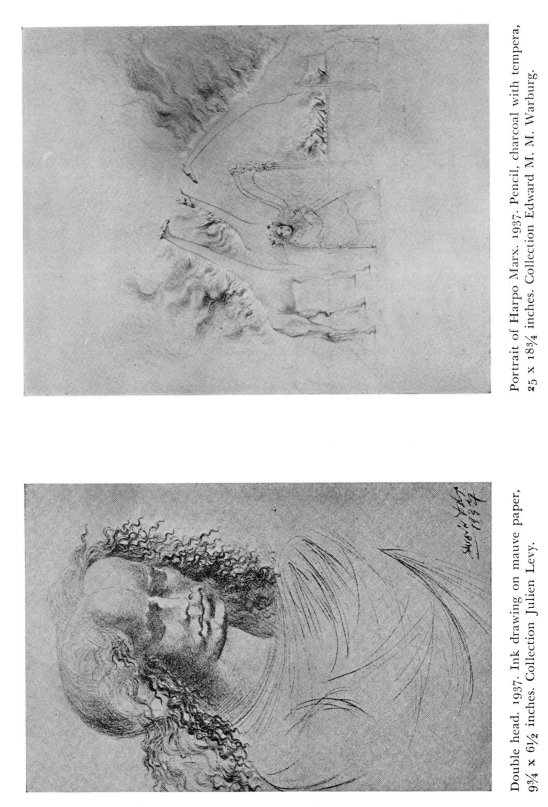

Portrait of Harpo Marx. 1937. Pencil, charcoal with tempera, 25 x 18¾ inches. Collection Edward M. M. Warburg.

Double head. 1937. Ink drawing on mauve paper, 9¾ x 6½ inches. Collection Julien Levy.

Figure of drawers. 1937. Ink drawing, 30¼ x 22⅝ inches. Collection Alfonso Gonzalez.

Figure. 1938. Ink drawing, 16¾ x 11¾ inches. Collection of the artist.

Marsupial figure. 1940. Ink drawing, 27¼ x 21¾
inches. Collection of the artist.

Hysterical arch. 1937. Ink drawing, 22 x 30⅛ inches. Collection Dr. Charles E. Roseman, Jr.

Landscape and anchorite. Ink and wash drawing.

The palace of Gala. Pencil.

90

The fountains. Ink drawing, 32¾ x 28¾ inches. Collection Mrs. S. Landau.

Backdrop for ballet *Bacchanale*.

92

Backdrop for ballet *Mad Tristan*.

Backdrop for ballet *Sentimental Colloquy*.

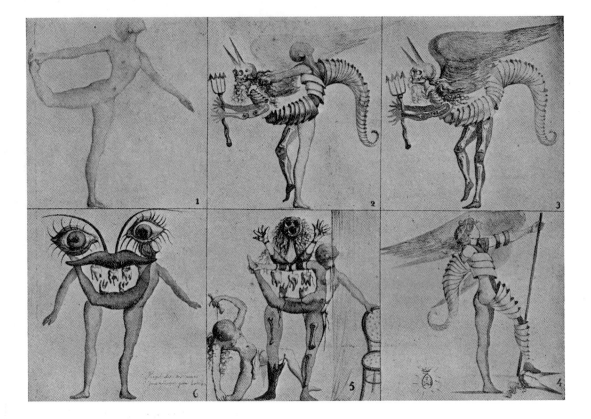

Costume designs for *Paranoiac Ballet*. Watercolor, 14½ x 22 inches. Collection Dr. Harry Lepman.

EXHIBITIONS BY DALI

EARLY GROUP SHOWS

1925 MADRID. Sociedad de Artistas Ibéricos. June-?.

1925 BARCELONA. Galeries Dalmau. Nov. 14-Dec. ? Sculpture by José Dunyac; drawings by Aurora Folquer and Salvador Dali.*

1926 BARCELONA. Circulo de Bellas Artes. Arte Catalán Moderno. Jan. 15-Feb.

1926 BARCELONA. Establiments Maragall. Fall (Saló de Tardor).

1926 BARCELONA. Galeries Dalmau. Fall (Saló d'Avantguarda).

1927 BARCELONA. Sala Parés. Fall (Saló de Tardor).

1927 BARCELONA. Galeries Dalmau. Drawings by Agustin Ferrer, Helios Goméz and Salvador Dali. Jan.*

1928 BARCELONA. Sala Parés. Fall (Saló de Tardor).

1928 BARCELONA. Galeries Dalmau. Winter (Inaugural).

1928 PITTSBURGH. Carnegie 27th International. Oct. 18-Dec. 18. 3 paintings.

ONE-MAN SHOWS

1929 PARIS. Galerie Goemans. Nov. 20-Dec. 5. 11 paintings, drawings.

1931 PARIS. Galerie Pierre Colle. June 3-15. 27 works, including paintings, objects.

1932 PARIS. Galerie Pierre Colle. May 26-June [1]7. 25 paintings, 2 objects.

1933 PARIS. Galerie Pierre Colle. June 19-29. 22 paintings, 10 drawings, objects.

1933 NEW YORK. Julien Levy Gallery. Nov. 21-Dec. 12. 25 paintings.

1933 BARCELONA. Galeria d'Art Catalònia. Dec. 8-21. 27 prints, 3 drawings, 2 paintings, 1 object, 6 photographs of varied works.

1934 NEW YORK. Julien Levy Gallery. Apr 3-[19?]. Drawings and etchings for *Les Chants de Maldoror.*

1934 PARIS. QUATRE CHEMINS. June 13-25. 42 etchings, 30 drawings for *Les Chants de Maldoror* (Editions Skira).

* For a part of the period specified, Dali's works may have been shown in a one-man exhibition.

1934 PARIS. Galerie Jacques Bonjean. June 20-July 13. 32 paintings, 2 sculptures, 4 objects, etchings for *Les Chants de Maldoror.*

1934 LONDON. Zwemmer Gallery. Oct. 24-Nov. 10. 16 paintings, 20 drawings, 17 etchings.

1934 NEW YORK. Julien Levy Gallery. Nov. 21-Dec. 10. 22 paintings.

1936 LONDON. Alex. Reid and Lefevre, Ltd. June-July. 29 paintings, 18 drawings.

1936-37 NEW YORK. Julien Levy Gallery. Dec. 15, 1936-Jan. 15, 1937. 21 paintings, 12 drawings.

1939 PARIS. [Salvador Dali's apartment.] Feb.

1939 NEW YORK. Julien Levy Gallery. Mar. 21-Apr. 18. 21 paintings, 5 drawings, objects.

1941 NEW YORK. Julien Levy Gallery. Apr. 22-May 31. 19 paintings, 3 portraits, drawings, 6 jewels, 1 crystal cup.
This exhibition subsequently shown, with minor modifications, by The Arts Club of Chicago (May 23-June 14), and by the Dalzell Hatfield Galleries, Los Angeles (Sept. 10-Oct. 5).

1941 HOLLYWOOD. Julien Levy Gallery. Oct. 15-22.

1941 NEW YORK. Museum of Modern Art. Nov. 19, 1941-Jan. 11, 1942. 50 paintings, 17 drawings, 6 jewels.

1943 NEW YORK. M. Knoedler and Co. Apr. 14-May 5. 20 paintings, 13 drawings.

1945 NEW YORK. Bignou Gallery. Nov. 20-Dec. 29. 11 paintings; drawings, illustrations and watercolors.

Sketch for a dream sequence in the motion picture, *Spellbound.*

95

FILMS IN WHICH DALI HAS COLLABORATED

Un Chien Andalou. Scenario by Luis Bunuel and Salvador Dali. Produced and directed by Luis Bunuel. Paris, 1929.

L'Age d'Or. Scenario by Luis Bunuel and Salvador Dali. Produced and directed by Luis Bunuel. Paris, 1931.

Spellbound. Produced by David O. Selznick, directed by Alfred Hitchcock. Dream sequences designed and executed by Salvador Dali. United Artists, 1945.

Destino. In production at Walt Disney Studios, Hollywood. Background paintings for cartoon by Salvador Dali. Disney Productions, 194?.

BALLETS IN WHICH DALI HAS COLLABORATED

BACCHANALE

Ballet in one act. Book: Salvador Dali. Music: Richard Wagner. Choreography: Leonide Massine. Scenery and costumes: Salvador Dali. Company: Ballet Theatre. Premiere: New York, 1939.

LABYRINTH

Ballet in four scenes. Book: Salvador Dali. Music: Franz Schubert. Choreography: Leonide Massine. Scenery and costumes: Salvador Dali. Company: Ballet Russe de Monte Carlo. Premiere: New York, 1941.

EL CAFE DE CHINITAS

A Quadro Flamenco. Book: Argentinita. Music: Spanish Folk arranged by Federico Garcia Lorca. Choreography: Argentinita. Curtain, scenery and costumes: Salvador Dali. Company: Ballet Theatre. Premiere: Detroit, Michigan, 1944.

SENTIMENTAL COLLOQUY

Music: Paul Bowles. Choreography: Andre Eglevsky. Scenery and costumes: Salvador Dali. Company: Ballet International. Premiere: New York, 1944.

MAD TRISTAN

The First Paranoic Ballet Based on the Eternal Myth of Love in Death, in two scenes. Book: Salvador Dali. Music: Richard Wagner. Choreography:

Leonide Massine. Curtain, scenery and costumes: Salvador Dali. Company: Ballet International. Premiere: New York, 1944.

JEWELRY BY DALI

Designed in collaboration with the Duke di Verdura. Cigarette box. 1941. Pale gold with jeweled beetle and painting on ivory.

Apollo and Daphne. 1941. Brooch, oil on gold, pink tourmaline; frame: gold, rubies, turquoises, 3 inches high.

Head of Medusa. 1941. Brooch, oil on gold, Morganite, gold, rubies, 2½ inches wide.

St. Sebastian. 1941. Object, oil on gold, petrified wood, agate, rubies, 5½ inches high.

Angel. 1941. Box, tourmaline, oil on ivory, gold, 2⅛ x 1⅝ inches.

Shell brooch with gold and diamonds. 1941. 3½ inches wide.

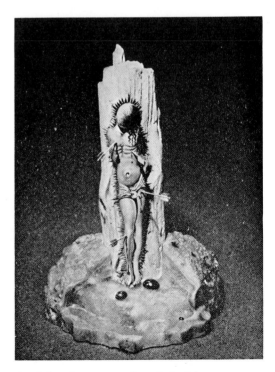

St. Sebastian. 1941. Jeweled object.

The arrangement, which is modeled upon that used by the Art Index, is alphabetically by author, or under the title in the case of unsigned articles. Publications of museums are entered under the name of the city in which the museum is located. Exhibition catalogs issued by private galleries are listed under the name of the gallery.

The bibliography proper has a supplement on book illustration by Dali, and a section on advertisements, sketches and designs. This revision is an enlargement of the 1941 list prepared for the first edition of the Dali catalog.

BERNARD KARPEL

ABBREVIATIONS: Ag *August*, Ap *April*, bibl *bibliography*, c *Copyright*, D *December*, ed *editor;* F *February*, il *illustration(s)*, Ja *January*, Je *June*, Jy *July*, My *May*, Mr *March*, N *November*, n.d. *not dated*, no(s) *number(s)*, O *October*, p *page(s)*, por *portrait(s)*, S *September*.

SAMPLE ENTRY: ALTMAN, GEORGES. La censure contre le cinéma: l'affaire de "L'Age d'or." 2il La Revue du Cinéma 3no19:40-2 F 1 1931. EXPLANATION: An article by Georges Altman, titled La censure contre le cinéma, etc., and containing 2 illustrations will be found in the periodical La Revue du Cinéma, volume 3, number 19, pages 40 to 42, issue dated February 1, 1931.

1. L'affaire de "'L'Age d'or." [6]p 4il [Privately published, 1931].

    Signed by Alexandre, Aragon, Breton, Char, Crevel, Dali and others. Originally published in bibl 101.

2. AGHA, MEHEMED FEHMY. Surrealism or the purple cow. 1il(por) Vogue p60-61,129-31,146 N 1 1936.

    Photograph of Dali by Cecil Beaton.

3. ALTMAN, GEORGES. La censure contre le cinéma: l'affaire de "L'Age d'or." 2il La Revue du Cinéma 3no19:40-2 F 1 1931.

4. The American cult for surrealism: Dali. 1il Art News 35:14 Ja 2 1937.

5. ARAGON, LOUIS. La peinture au défi. Exposition de collages, Arp, Braque, Dali [etc.], mars 1930. p27-8 1il Paris, Corti, 1930.

    ARTS CLUB OF CHICAGO. See bibl 172.

6. BALAKIAN, ANNA. The metaphysical gamut of surrealism. French Review 18no4:202-8 F 1945.

7. BALLET INTERNATIONAL, NEW YORK. Program magazine. p12-4 [O 30 1944].

    Data on *Sentimental Colloquy* and illustration for *Mad Tristan*.

8. Ballet Russe. The Studio 120no572:162-7 N 1940.

    Includes color design for *Bacchanale*.

9. BALLET RUSSE DE MONTE CARLO. [Souvenir programme, 1939-40]. 5il New York, 1939.

    Includes synopsis and designs, some in color, for *Bacchanale*.

10. ———— [Souvenir programme]. 6il New York, 1942.

    Includes synopsis and designs for *Labyrinth*.

10a. BALTIMORE MUSEUM OF ART. Foreign section 1934. Carnegie international exhibition of paintings, January fourth-February twelfth MCMXXXV. 1il p15 Baltimore, 1935.

    BARR, ALFRED H., JR. See bibl 188, 190.

11. BARRY, IRIS. Hidden faces, by Salvador Dali [review]. New York Herald Tribune Je 11 1944.

12. BATAILLE, GEORGES. Dictionnaire: oeil. 3il Documents no4:216 S 1929.

    Horror of the eye, exemplified in *Un Chien Andalou*. English digest, p[235].

13. ———— Le jeu lugubre. 1il Documents no7:369-72 D 1929.

    BAZIN, GERMAIN. See bibl 154.

14. BEATON, CECIL. Time exposure. With commentary and captions by Peter Quennell. p33 3il (por) New York, Charles Scribner's Sons, 1941.

15. BENET, RAFAEL. La vida artística. Ciutat 1no8: 205 S-D 1926.

    Review of the Saló de Tardor at Establiments Maragall and the Saló d'Avantguarda at the Galeries Dalmau.

16. ———— La vida artística. 2il Ciutat 2no15: 162 O-D 1927.

    "El Saló de Tardor organitzat per Joan A. Maragall a can Parés."

17. ———— La vida artística. 1il Ciutat 2no9: 19 Ja 1927.

    Exhibition of Salvador Dali at the Galeries Dalmau.

17a. ———— La vida artística. Ciutat 2no13: 110 Je 1927.
Apparently a student production in Barcelona of Garcia Lorca's *Mariana Pineda*, the stage designs for which were executed by Dali. (Also mentioned in bibl 115.)

17b. ———— A l'entorn de la inaugural de can Dalmau. 1il Gaseta de les Arts (2 series) 1no3:8, 12 N 1928.

18. BERGER, ARTHUR V. Dali's "Tristan" in its premiere. New York Sun D 16 1944.

19. BERNERS, LORD. Surrealist landscape. Horizon 6no31:5-6 Jy 1942.
Poem dedicated to Salvador Dali.

20. BIGNOU GALLERY, NEW YORK. Recent paintings by Salvador Dali, November 20th-December 29th, 1945. 17p 7il [New York, 1945].
Foreword and captions to illustrations by Dali.

21. BILLE, EJLER. Picasso, surrealisme, abstrakt kunst. p192-3, 204-12 6il(por) [Copenhagen] Forlget Helios, 1945.

21a. BJERKE-PETERSEN, VILHELM. Surrealismen. 2il p71, 92-3 Kobenhavn, Nordlundes Bogtrykkeri, n.d. (Linien's bibliotek. nr.1).

22. BLAKESTON, OSWELL. Paris shorts and longs. Close Up 5 no2:143-4 Ag 1929.
Comment on *Un Chien Andalou*. (Two stills in the following issue, S 1929.) Additional notes by Jean Lenauer Close Up 6no2:138-9 F 1930, and by John C. Moore Close Up 9no4: 282 D 1932.

23. BLOCK, MAXINE, ed. Dali, Salvador. 1il(por) Current Biography 1:219-21 1940.
Includes bibliography.

24. BLUNT, ANTHONY. Another superrealist. Spectator 157:57 Jy 10 1936.

25. BOR, VANE. Correspondance à Salvador Dali, Beograd, 31 décembre 1932. Le Surréalisme au Service de la Révolution no6:46-7 1933.

26. BOSTON, MODERN INSTITUTE OF ART. Four Spaniards: Dali, Gris, Miro, Picasso. January 24-March 3, 1946. [Boston, 1946].
Exhibition catalog with brief comment, listing 19 paintings by Dali.

27. BOSWELL, PEYTON, JR. Is Dali crazy? Art Digest 15no15:3 My 1 1941.

28. BRETON, ANDRÉ. Surréalisme et la peinture, suivi de Genèse et perspective artistiques du surréalisme et de Fragments inédits. p144-7, passim New York, Brentano's, 1945.

29. ———— What is surrealism? p27-30, 82-4 London, Faber & Faber, 1936.
Incorporates *Qu'est-ce que le surréalisme?* Bruxelles, René Henriquez, 1934, originally a lecture at Brussels. *The first Dali exhibition*, p27-30, is a translation of his introduction to the Goemans catalog of 1929 (bibl 144).

———— See also bibl 199, 235-7.

30. BRUNIUS, J. BERNARD. Un chien andalou, par Louis Bunuel (Studio-film). La Revue du Cinéma 1no4:67-8 O 15 1929.

31. BRUSSELS. ECRAN DU SÉMINAIRE DES ARTS. Programme: L'Age d'or. [4]p Bruxelles, Harry Fishman, 1945.
"Les jeudis 21 et 28 juin 1945 en la Salle de Musique de Chambre du Palais des Beaux-Arts."

32. BULLIET, CLARENCE JOSEPH. The significant moderns and their pictures. p129-30 1il New York, Covici-Friede, 1936.

BUNUEL, LUIS. See bibl 101, 102.

32a. CABOT, JUST. Saló de tardor. 1il Gaseta de les Arts (2 series) 1no3:14 N 1928.
Additional notes on p7, and in 1no2:48 O 1928.

33. CALAS, NICOLAS. Anti-surrealist Dali: I say his flies are ersatz. View 1no6:1,3 Je 1941.

34. ———— Confound the wise. p203, 206, 243-4, 247 New York, Arrow Editions, 1942.

35. CARNEGIE INSTITUTE, PITTSBURGH. Twenty-seventh annual international exhibition of paintings. [Pittsburgh, 1928].
Catalog of an exhibition held October 18-December 18. Nos 361, 362, 363 by Salvador Dali y Domenech.

———— See also 10a.

36. El casa del film surrealista "La edad de oro" en Tenerife. Gaceta de Arte 4no36:2 O 1935.

37. CASSANYES, MAGÍ A. Dali. 3il(1col) D'Ací i D'Allà 22no179:[60-1] D 1934.

38. ———— L'Espai en les pintures de Salvador Dali. 2il L'Amic de les Arts 2no13:30-1 Ap 30 1927.

39. CASSOU, JEAN. La jeune peinture espagnol. 1il La Renaissance 16:162-3 Jy 1933.

———— See also bibl 154.

39a. Castleton china exhibit here hailed as a thrilling adventure in ceramics. 1il Indianapolis Sunday Star p17 Ap 18 1943.

40. CHAMPIGNEULLE, BERNARD. L'Inquiétude dans l'art d'aujourd'hui. 2il L'Amour de l'Art 18n01:17-22 Ja 1937; 18n03:77-82 Mr 1937.

41. CHAVANCE, LOUIS. Les influence de L'Age d'or. La Revue du Cinéma 3n019:48-50 F 1 1931.

42. CHERONNET, LOUIS. Salvador Dali. Art et Décoration 63:280 Jy 1934.

43. Closeup of the Dali technique; or, what sitters get for their money. 2il Art News 42:11 Ap 15 1943.

44. CLOUD, Y. A note on the affair of the surrealist film L'Age d'or. [4]p [1931?].
Private publication included in Documents 1930-1934 (bibl 218).

45. COLLE, PIERRE, GALERIE, PARIS. Exposition Salvador Dali, du 3 au 15 juin 1931. [6]p 2il Paris, Imprimerie des Galeries Georges Petit, 1931.
Exhibition catalog, with note by S. Dali, p[3-4]: Surtout, l'art ornamental. . . .

46. —————— Exposition Salvador Dali, du 26 mai au [1]7 juin 1932. [7]p 1il [Paris, 1932].
Salvador Dali, poem by Paul Eluard, p1-4.

47. —————— Exposition Salvador Dali, du 19 au 23 juin. [10]p 1il [Paris, 1933].
Catalog of an exhibition, with frontispiece drawing by Dali and his preface dedicated to Breton, 6p. Extract from preface printed as note in Julien Levy catalog (bibl 169).

47a. CONNOLLY, CYRIL. The unquiet grave; a word cycle by Palinurus. p123-5 New York and London, Harper & Brothers, 1945.
Summary of and commentary on Un Chien Andalou.

48. CORDAN, WOLFGANG. Essai over het surrealisme. p11-2,17 Amsterdam, Mij Contact, 1935.

49. CREVEL, RENÉ. Dali; ou, L'anti-obscurantisme. 30p plus 10 plates Paris, Editions Surréalistes, 1931.
Also issued in de luxe edition (bibl 239).
—————— See also bibl 103.

50. DALI, SALVADOR. The abject misery of abstraction-creation. See bibl 56.
—————— Un album de 6 photographies des tableaux de Salvador Dali. Paris, Corti, 1932.
—————— L'Amour. See bibl 66.

51. —————— L'Amour et la mémoire. 1il(por) Paris, Editions Surréalistes, 1931.
Translated on p145-6 of Gascoyne (bibl 141) and on p158-9 of Levy (bibl 167).

52. —————— L'Ane pourri. Le Surréalisme au Service de la Révolution no1:9-12 1930.
Subsequently published in La femme visible (bibl 66). Translated by J. Bronowski as The stinking ass This Quarter 5n01:49-54 S 1932.
—————— L'Angélus de Millet. See bibl 210.

53. —————— Apparitions aérodynamiques des "Etres-objets." 5il Minotaure no 6:33-4 1935.

54. —————— Babaouo; scénario inédit. Précédé d'un abrégé d'une histoire critique du cinéma, et suivi de Guillaume Tell, ballet portugais. 58p Paris, Editions des Cahiers Libres, 1932.
Fragment translated by Julien Levy (bibl 167).
—————— [The ballet Bacchanale.] See bibl 148.
—————— La chèvre sanitaire. See bibl 66.

55. —————— Communication: visage paranoïaque. 3il Le Surréalisme au Service de la Révolution no3:[40] 1931.

56. —————— Conquest of the irrational. 32p plus 35 plates (1col) New York, Julien Levy, 1935.
Contents: The waters in which we swim, p7-11.—My pictorial struggle, p11-8.—The abject misery of abstraction-creation, p19-23.—The tears of Heraclitus, p24-5. Translated by David Gascoyne. Also issued in de luxe edition (bibl 240).

57. —————— Cradled pamphlet. Contemporary Poetry and Prose no2:29 Je 1936.
Translated by A. L. Lloyd. Also translated by Julien Levy (bibl 167) as Binding cradled-cradle bound.

58. —————— La dada fotogràfica. 4il Gaseta de les Arts 2n06:40-2 F 1929.
—————— Dali, Dali! See bibl 171.

59. —————— Dali news, monarch of the dailies, vol.1, no.1, New York, Tuesday, November 20, 1945. [4]p [Privately published, 1945.]
Illustrated newssheet issued in conjunction with the Bignou exhibition. Includes comments on Spellbound, ballet, etc.
—————— Dali to the reader. See bibl 162.

60. —————— De la beauté terrifiante et comestible de l'architecture 'modern' style. 17il Minotaure no3-4:69-76 1933.

61. —————— Declaration of the independence of the imagination and the rights of man to his

own madness. [4]p 1il [Privately published, 1939].

Partly reprinted in *Dali manifests* Art Digest 13:9 Ag 1939.

62. ———— Derniers modes d'excitation intellectuelle pour l'été 1934. Documents 34no1:33-5 Je 1934.

63. ———— Dictionnaire abrégé du surréalisme. See bibl 112.

64. ———— Dues proses. L'Amic de les Arts 2no20:104 N 30 1927.

65. ———— Les eaux où nous nageons. Cahiers d'Art 10no5-6:122-4 1935.
Translated by David Gascoyne (bibl 56).

66. ———— La femme visible. 78p 10il Paris, Editions Surréalistes, 1930.

With 3 etchings by Dali. Contents: L'Ane pourri, p11-20.—La chèvre sanitaire, p23-34.—Le grand masturbateur, p37-60.—L'Amour, p65-71.

———— Foreword [and captions to illustrations]. See bibl 20.

67. ———— La fotografia pura creació de l'esprit. L'Amic de les Arts 2no18:90-1 S 30 1927.

———— Geological foundations of Venusberg. See bibl 178.

———— Le grand masturbateur. See bibl 66.

68. ———— Hidden faces. Translated by Haakon M. Chevalier. 413p 3il(1col) New York, Dial Press, 1944.

Colored book-jacket and 2 illustrations by Dali. Translator's foreword, pvii-xi.

69. ———— Honneur à l'objet! 3il Cahiers d'Art 11no1-2:53-7 1936.

Analyse de "L'Escalier de l'Amour et Psyché" inventé para Gala—Analyse du veston aphrodisiaque de Salvador Dali, p57.

70. ———— I defy Aragon. Art Front 3no2:7-8 Mr 1937.

71. ———— Les idées lumineuses. Cahiers d'Art 15no1-2:24-5 1940.

72. ———— Interprétation paranoïaque — critique de l'image obsédante "L'Angélus" de Millet. Minotaure no1:65-7 1933.

Manuscript outline for a work of the same title is included in *Documents 1930-1934* (bibl 218). Announcement of publication by Editions Surréalistes printed in Le Surréalisme au Service de la Révolution no6:[iii] 1933.

73. ———— Joan Miro. L'Amic de les Arts 3no26:202 Je 30 1938.

74. ———— [Manifesto. 1928.]
Reference from Enciclopedia Universal Ilustrada (bibl 115): "En marzo de 1928 publico un manifesto con Gasch y Montanyá."

75. ———— La métamorphose de Narcisse; poème paranoïaque. Paris, Editions Surréalistes, 1936.

English translation by Francis Scarpe: Metamorphosis of Narcissus. 20p 4il(1col) New York, Julien Levy, 1937. Cover photograph by Cecil Beaton.

———— My pictorial struggle. See bibl 56.

76. ———— New York salutes me. 5il Spain 6no7:10-1, 23 My 1941.

Includes critical note by the editor. Text also issued as broadside with same title, signed *Dali*.

———— [Note: this exhibition of my paintings.] See bibl 169.

77. ———— Notes—communications. Le Surréalisme au Service de la Révolution no6:40-1 1933.

78. ———— Notes pour l'interprétation du tableau "La persistence de la mémoire." [1]p n.d.

Manuscript (photostat in Library of the Museum of Modern Art).

79. ———— Nous límits de la pinture. L'Amic de les Arts 3no22:167-9 F 29 1928.

80. ———— Les nouvelles couleurs du sex appeal spectral. 6il Minotaure no5:20-2 1934.

81. ———— The object as revealed in surrealist experiment. This Quarter 5no1:197-207 S 1932.

Translated by David Gascoyne, who also includes a partial translation in his survey (bibl 141). The foot-note *Typical surrealist objects operating symbolically* (p205-6 above) is a partial translation of bibl 83.

82. ———— Objects psycho-atmosphériques-anamorphiques. 1il Le Surréalisme au Service de la Révolution no5:45-8 1933.

83. ———— Objects surréalistes. Le Surréalisme au Service de la Révolution no3:16-7 1931.
Summarized and partly translated in Gascoyne (bibl 141) and in This Quarter (bibl 81).

84. ———— Painting after the tempest. 1il (col) Harper's Bazaar 80no2:128-9 F 1946. Translated by Elaine Shaplen.

85. ———— Les pantoufles de Picasso. Cahiers d'Art 10no7-10:208, 210, 212 1935.

86. ————Peix perseguit per un raün. L'Amic de les Arts 3no28:217-8 S 31 1928.

87. ———— Le phénomène de l'extase. 2il Minotaure no3-4:76-7 1933.

88. ———— Poema de les cosettes. L'Amic de les Arts 3no27:211 Ag 31 1928.

———— [Preface, dedicated to Breton.] See bibl 47.

89. ———— Première loi morphologique sur les poils dans les structures molles. 1il Minotaure no9:60-1 1936.

90. ———— Psychologie non-euclidienne d'une photographie. 1il Minotaure no7:56-7 1935.

91. ———— ¿Que he renegat, potser? L'Amic de les Arts 3no30:233 D 31 1928.

92. ———— Reflexions. L'Amic de les Arts 2no17:69 Ag 31 1927.

93. ———— Rêverie. Le Surréalisme au Service de la Révolution no 4:31-6 1931.

94. ———— Sant Sebastià. 1il L'Amic de les Arts 2no16:52-4 Jy 31 1927.

95. ———— Secret life of Salvador Dali. Click 5no9:34-7 S 1942. "Staged and edited by Dali," with sketches and photographs.

96. ———— The secret life of Salvador Dali. Translated by Haakon M. Chevalier. 400p New York, Dial Press, 1942. Profusely illustrated, with 3 colored plates and colored book-jacket. Excerpts published in Town and Country 7il(1col) 96:54-7, 94, 96-8 My 1941, and facsimile fragment in Levy folio catalog (bibl 172).

———— [Si je dois m'exprimer brièvement sur les questions du "modèle" . . .] See bibl 220.

———— Surrealism [euphonic announcement]. See bibl 167.

97. ———— Le surréalisme spectral de l'éternal féminin préraphaélite. Minotaure no8:46-9 1936.

———— The tears of Heraclitus. See bibl 56.

98. ———— [Telegram: an explanation of the painting "The persistence of memory."] 1il Life 19no16:9-10 O 15 1945.

———— [Surtout, l'art ornamental . . .] See bibl 45.

99. ———— Temes actual. 2il L'Amic de les Arts 2no19:98-9 O 31 1927.

100. ———— Total camouflage for total war. 13il(2col) Esquire 18no2:64-6, 129-30 Ag 1942. Includes A portrait of Salvador Dali by Salvador Dali (p130). Translated by Florence Gilliam.

———— You could see the ass's bone. See bibl 167.

———— See also bibl 105, 109, 113, 114, 233.

101. ———— and BUNUEL, LUIS. L'Age d'or. 38p including plates 2il Paris, Corti, 1931. Contents: Note by Dali, p1.—Le scénario, p2-7.—L'Age d'Or, signed by Alexandre, Aragon, Breton, Char, Crevel, Dali, etc., p17-9.—Stills, p22-37. Lettered on rear cover: Studio 28, revue-programme. A private publication (bibl 1) containing text from p1-3, 17-9 is included in Documents 1930-1934 (bibl 218); 4 stills reproduced in Le Surréalisme au Service de la Révolution no1 1930.

102. ———— and BUNUEL, LUIS. Un chien andalou. La Révolution Surréaliste no12:34-7 D 15 1929. A translation from the Spanish by Maxime Zvoinski Un chien andalou; scénario de Louis Bunuel et Salvador Dali appeared in Revue du Cinéma 1no5:3-16 N 15 1929. A translation by Richard Thoma The Andalusian dog was published in This Quarter 5no1:149-57 S 1932, and also in Levy (bibl 167). Two stills from the film reproduced in Les Cahiers Jaunes no4:22 1933; a larger selection accompanies the Zvoinski translation.

103. ———— and CREVEL, RENÉ. Per un tribunal terrorista de responsabilitats intelectuals. Barcelona, La Hora, 1931.

104. Dali and Miro jar New York with visions of the subconscious. 2il Art Digest 16no5:5-6 D 1 1941. Review of exhibition at the Museum of Modern Art.

105. Dali proclaims surrealism a paranoiac art. 1il Art Digest 9no9:10 F 1 1935.
      Summarizes lecture at the Museum of Modern Art, with quotations.

106. Dali throws a daffy party. 9il Look 5no23:50-3 N 18 1941.

107. Dali, surrealist, has a nightmare while wide awake. New York World-Telegram p17 Mr 17 1939.
      Account of Dali's window display at Bonwit-Teller.

108. Dali's dream of ballet: Labyrinth . . . second ballet in the trilogy by the great surrealist painter. 7il Vogue p34-5 D 15 1941.

109. Dali's heterosexual monster invades Chicago. 1il Art Digest18no2:13 O 15 1943.
      Quotes telegraphed explanation by Dali.

110. DENBY, EDWIN. Dali to the hilt. New York Herald Tribune D 16 1944.
      Review of the ballet Mad Tristan.

111. D[EVREE], H[OWARD]. Portraits by Dali. 5il New York Times Magazine p17 Ap 11 1943.
      Review of Knoedler exhibition.

112. DICTIONNAIRE ABRÉGÉ DU SURRÉALISME. 76p including plates Paris, Galerie Beaux-Arts, 1938.
      Numerous definitions by Dali, signed S. D. Supplement: Exposition internationale du surréalisme, janvier-février 1938. (Nos. 43-50 by Dali.)

113. DOMINGUEZ, OSCAR. Carta de Paris; conversación con Salvador Dali. 1il Gaceta de Arte 3no28:3 1934.

114. DU TEMPS QUE LES SURRÉALISTES AVAIENT RAISON. 15p Paris, Editions Surréalistes, 1935.
      Essay signed by Breton, Dali, Eluard, Ernst and others.

ELUARD, PAUL. See bibl 46, 199, 237, 242.

115. ENCICLOPEDIA UNIVERSAL ILUSTRADA EUROPEO-AMERICANA. Dalí (Salvador). (Apéndice)3:1403 Bilbao, Madrid, Barcelona, Espasa-Calpe, 1931.
      Dali's early life and work, 1921-1928.

115a. FARBER, MANNY. Dream manors [review of "Spellbound"]. The New Republic p747 D 3 1945.

115b. FARNER, KONRAD. Hans Erni. 1il p41-2 Basel-Zürich, Mundus Verlag, 1945.

116. FERNANDEZ, JUSTINO. Prometeo, ensayo sobre pintura contemporánea. p65-76 1il México, D. F., Editorial Porrua, 1945.

117. FILM SOCIETY, NEW YORK. The Film society presents Luis Bunuel's surrealist film "L'Age d'or." Programme 3, March 19th, 1933. [4]p [New York, 1933].
      Includes a commentary and synopsis.

117a. FLAMA, ————. Els de les "Arts i els artistes." 1il(por) Gaseta de les Arts 4no69:1-2 Mr 15 1927.
      Includes group photograph with Dali in background.

118. FOIX, J. V. Presentació de Salvador Dali. 2il L'Amic de les Arts 2no10:3 Ja 31 1927.

119. FOLCH I TORRES, JOAQUIM. El pintor Salvador Dali. 1il Gaseta de les Arts 3no6:2 N 1 1926.

120. ———— Salvador Dali. 3il Gaseta de les Arts 4no66:1-2 F 1 1927.

121. 14,400 Dali ties. Art Digest 18no20:7 S 1 1944.
      Tie patterns for McCurrach, a reproduction of which appeared in Esquire p37 O 1944.

122. FRANCÉS, JOSÉ. El año artístico, 1925-1926. p238, 246 Barcelona, Editorial Lux, 1928.

123. FRANCISCO, ESTEBAN. Dali, centro de innumerables controversias. 3il(col) Norte 5no10:33-5 Ag 1945.

123a. FRANSK SURREALISM. 1il p43-51 Stockholm, Spektrum, 1933 (Nya strömningar).

124. Freud + Minsky = Dali. Art Digest 13:12 Jy 1 1939.
      Description of World's Fair show. (Photographs showing pavilion in construction in possession of J. T. Soby.)

125. FREY, J. G. From dada to surrealism. 1il Parnassus 8no7:15 D 1936.

126. FRICK REFERENCE LIBRARY, NEW YORK. [Salvador Dali reproductions.] n.d.
      Portfolio of mounted, classified, and sourced illustrations of the work of Dali including sketches, advertisements, etc.

127. FROIS-WITTMANN, JEAN. L'art moderne et le principe du plaisir. Minotaure 1no3-4:79-80 D 1933.
      See reference to this article by Kayser, p45 (bibl 161). A more general study by Frois-Wittmann is Preliminary psychoanalytical considerations of modern art Archives of Psychoanalysis 1 part 4 Jy 1 1927.

128. Frozen nightmares. Time 24no22:44-5 N 26 1934.

129. FURST, HERBERT. Art notes . . . sanity or insanity in art. Apollo 24no140:111-2 Ag 1936.
Includes review of Dali show at Reid and Lefevre.

130. ———— Is art taking a wrong turning? Apollo 41:122-4 My 1945.

131. ———— Notes of the month: Salvador Dali at the Zwemmer galleries. Apollo 20no 120:348 D 1934.

132. GALERIE D'ART CATALÒNIA, BARCELONA. Salvador Dali. [4]p 1il(por) 1933.
Catalog of an exhibition held December 8-21, with Dali photo by Man Ray on cover.

133. GALERIE DE ARTE MEXICANO, MEXICO CITY. Exposicion internacional del surrealismo, enero-febrero 1940. Organizadores: André Breton, Wolfgang Paalen, César Moro. 1il [Mexico City, 1940].
Illustrated catalog, with text in Spanish and English. Nos. 23-7 by Dali.

133a. GALERIES DALMAU [EXPOSICIÓ DALÍ]. Gaseta de les Arts 2no28:6-7 D 1 1925.

GARCÍA LORCA, FEDERICO. See bibl 17a, 147.

134. GASCH, SEBASTIÀ. L'Exposció collectiva de la sala Parés. L'Amic de les Arts 2no19:95 O 31 1927.

135. ———— Inaugural de les galeries Dalmau. L'Amic de les Arts 3no30:236-8 D 31 1928.

135a. ———— La pintura catalana contemporánea. p6,21,24-6 Barcelona, Comissariat de Propaganda de la Generalitat de Catalunya, 1937. (Aspectos de la actividad catalana. 4.)

136. ———— Salvador Dali. 2il L'Amic de les Arts 1no8:4, 6 N 1926.

137. ———— Salvador Dali. 1il Gaseta de les Arts 3no6:1-2 N 1 1926.

138. ———— Salvador Dali. 4il Ciutat 2no10: 31-4 F 1927.

139. ———— Salvador Dali. 2il L'Amic de les Arts 2no11:16-7 F 28 1927.

140. ———— Salvador Dali. 5il Cahiers de Belgique 3no4:126-30 1930.

141. GASCOYNE, DAVID. A short survey of surrealism. p91-110, passim London, Cobden-Sanderson, 1936.
Extract from *The object as revealed in surrealist experiment*, p99, 101.—Summary of *Objets surréalistes*, p108-9.—Fragment from *Love and memory*, p145-6.

142. GAUNT, WILLIAM. Art's nightmare: the surrealist paintings of Salvador Dali. 4il(1col) London Studio 18:108-13 S 1939.

143. GAUSS, CHARLES E. The theoretical backgrounds of surrealism. Journal of Aesthetics 2no8:37-44 1943.
Brief inspection of "the scriptural texts of the two leading surrealists, André Breton and Salvator Dali."

144. GOEMANS, GALERIE, PARIS. Dali . . . du 20 novembre au décembre 1929. [6]p 3il [Paris, 1929].
Exhibition catalog, with preface on Dali by André Breton, p1, 3 (translated in bibl 29).

145. GEORGE, WALDEMAR. Avant son départ pour New York, Salvador Dali a presenté dans son atelier un choix de ses oeuvres. Beaux-Arts p4 F 10 1939.

146. George Platt Lynes "Dream of Venus." 1il(por) U. S. Camera 1no5:42 Ag 1939.
World's Fair issue, reproducing with brief comment, Lynes' "lobster & nude" portrait of Dali.

147. GÓMEZ DE LA SERNA, RAMÓN. Ismos.p421-40 9il(1col) Buenos Aires, Editorial Poseidon, 1943.
Federico García Lorca *Oda a Salvador Dali* p432-6.

148. GOODE, GERALD. The book of ballets, classic and modern. p19-20 2il(col) New York, Crown Publishers, 1939.
The ballet *Bacchanale*, including description by Salvador Dali.
GUGLIELMI, LOUIS. See bibl 183.

149. HARRIMAN, MARGARET CASE. Profiles: a dream walking. New Yorker 15:22-7 Jy 1 1939.

150. HARTLEY, MARSDEN. The spangle of existence: casual dissertations. p[101-5] [1942].
Essay titled *Sur-realism—and Dali, or—disorderly house* from unpublished typescript in the Museum of Modern Art library.
HATFIELD, DALZELL, GALLERIES, LOS ANGELES. See bibl 172.

151. HILAIRE, G. Chez les surréalistes: Salvador Dali. 1il Beaux-Arts p2 Je 30 1933.
Review of Pierre Colle exhibition.

152. HOPPER, HEDDA. Hollywood [Disney and Dali confer on "Destino" cartoon]. New York Daily News p44 Ja 31, 1946.

153. How super-realist Dali saw Broadway. American Weekly p5 Mr 5 1935.
Includes drawings made for this Sunday section of the New York Journal-American.
HUGNET, GEORGES. See bibl 188, 199, 244.

154. HUYGHE, RENÉ, ed. Histoire de l'art contemporain: la peinture. p340, 342-3 Paris, Alcan, 1935.

Essay by Jean Cassou *Le dadaïsme et le surréalisme*, article by Germain Bazin *Notice historique sur dada et le surréalisme,* and bibliographical note by Bazin on Dali, reprinted from L'Amour de l'Art 15:337-343 Mr 1934.

155. IBERO, SANTIAGO. Contemporary Spanish art. Art and Archaeology 25no1:54, 57 Ja 1928.

156. INTERNATIONAL BUSINESS MACHINES CORPORATION, NEW YORK. Contemporary art of 79 countries . . . exhibited . . . at the Golden Gate international exposition, San Francisco, Cal. p[138-9] 2il(por) [New York, 1939].

157. ISAACS, WALTER. What kind of surrealism? College Art Journal 3no2:46-51 Ja 1944.
JACINTO, FELIPE. See bibl 172.

157a. JAMES, EDWARD. [Anecdotes of Dali's childhood, dictated by Edward James at the Museum of Modern Art.] [4]p 1944.

Typescript in the possession of J. T. Soby. Copy in the Museum of Modern Art Library.

——————— See also bibl 245.

157b. JANIS, HARRIET. Paintings as a key to psychoanalysis. 1il Arts & Architecture 63no2:38-40, 60 F 1946.

Includes a detailed analysis of Dali's *Illumined Pleasures* (1929).

158. ——————— Abstract & surrealist art in America. p7, 8, 28, 86, 126, 140 2il(1col) New York, Reynal & Hitchcock, 1944.

159. JANIS, SIDNEY. Journey into a painting by Ernst, 1il *View* 2no1:10,12 Ap 1942.

160. JEWELL, EDWARD ALDEN. Dali, an enigma?—only his exegesis. New York Times p19 N 21 1945.

Review of Bignou exhibition.

161. KAYSER, STEPHEN S. Salvador Dali's search for heaven. 8il Pacific Art Review 2no3-4:30-56 winter 1942-43.

"References," p54-6.

162. KNOEDLER, M. AND CO., NEW YORK. Dali, April 14 to May 5, 1943. 12p plus 25 plates [New York, Art Aid Corporation, 1943].

Dali to the reader, p[1-5].

162a. KRAUS, H. FELIX. The easel: modern art, 1945. 2il Tricolor 3no13:48 Ap 1945.

163. LACAN, JACQUES. De la psychose paranoïaque dans ses rapports avec le personalité. 381p Paris, Le François, 1932.

163a. ——————— Le problème du style et la conception psychiatrique des formes paranoïaques de l'expérience. Minotaure no1:68-9 1933.

164. LAPRADE, J. DE. Salvador Dali. Beaux-Arts p1 Je 19 1934.

165. LARREA, JUAN. El surrealism entre viejo y nuevo mundo. 2il Cuadernos Americanos 16 no4:221,223 Jy-Ag 1944.

166. LEMAITRE, GEORGES. From cubism to surrealism in French literature. 2il p208,214,223 Cambridge, Mass., Harvard University Press, 1941.

167. LEVY, JULIEN. Surrealism. 191p 8il New York, Black Sun Press, 1936.

Partial contents: Salvador Dali, p23-5.—[The surrealist cinema] p65.—An Andalusian dog, p66-72. Translated by Richard Thoma.—L'Age d'or, p73-4.—Babaouo (fragment), p75-6. Translated by J. L.—Binding cradled-cradle bound (poem), p157. Translated by J. L.—Love and memory (fragment), p158-9. Translated by J. L.—Surrealism (euphonic announcement by Dali), p160.—William Tell (A Portuguese ballet), p161-2. Translated by J. L.—You could see the ass's bone (poem). Translated by Wayne Andrews, p163-4.

168. LEVY, JULIEN, GALLERY, NEW YORK. Le chien andalou [advertisement]. 193?.

Small sheet announcing film available for rental, with note by Luis Bunuel.

169. ——————— Exhibition of paintings by Salvador Dali, November 21st to December 8th. 2il [New York, 1933].

Catalog listing 25 paintings by Dali, 1 by Hieronymus Bosch, with drawing and note by Dali partly translated from the introduction to the Colle 1933 catalog (bibl 47).

170. ——————— Dali paints the invisible straight from nature. [2]p [New York, 1936].

Souvenir catalog issued for an exhibition held Dec. 15, 1936-Jan. 15, 1937. Catalog on reverse of stiff board. "The front represents a female half-nude, whose breasts can be opened by way of metal-snaps to release two miniature accordion-pleated strips of reproductions of Dali's work." Printed in France. (*Art nouveau* bed announcement, dated Dec. 10, was designed as invitation to this exhibition.)

171. ——————— Salvador Dali, 1939. [4]p [New York, 1939].
Catalog for an exhibition held March 21-April 18. Cover design by Dali, also preface *Dali, Dali!* Reproduction of *The Endless Enigma* with 6 analytical drawings and 6 separate drawings on tracing paper for superimposition.

172. ——————— Salvador Dali, April 22-May 31 1941. [6]p [New York, 1941].
Exhibition catalog, with essay by Felipe Jacinto *The last scandal of Salvador Dali* translated by Julien Levy. Reissued with modifications by the Arts Club of Chicago and the Dalzell Hatfield Galleries to accompany their showings of the exhibition. Also in folio edition on stiff board with facsimile fragment from the manuscript of "Secret life of Salvador Dali."

173. LÓPEZ TORRES, DOMINGO. Lo real y lo superreal en la pintura de Salvador Dalí. 2il Gaceta de Arte no28:1-2 Jy 1934.
Includes bibliography.

173a. LOVEMAN, HILDA. Other news on the award front. MKR's Art Outlook no8:7 Mr 1946.
Dali, Ernst and others painting *The Temptation of St. Anthony* for forthcoming film version of Maupassant's *Bel Ami* (Loew-Levin production).

174. Mad "dream betrayal" of New York society at the astounding party to its newest idol. New York Mirror p10-1 F 24 1935.
Illustrated news account for the Sunday magazine section.

175. MANN, KLAUS. Surrealist circus. American Mercury 56no230:174-81 F 1943.
Excerpts in Art Digest 17:21 My 15 1943, and reply in 17:4 Je 1943.

176. MARTIN, JOHN. Surrealist painter's version of Venusberg scene from "Tannhaeuser" presented. New York Times p26 N 10 1939.

176a. Marvelous and fantastic. 3il(por) Time 28no24:60-2 D 14 1936.
Review of Fantastic Art exhibition at the Museum of Modern Art, with special emphasis on Dali, and Man Ray photo of Dali on magazine cover.

176b. MELTZOFF, STANLEY. David Smith and social realism. 1il Magazine of Art 39no3:98-9 Mr 1946.
Brief analysis of Dali's *Uranium and Atomica Melancholia Idyll.*

177. Meshes of Anamorphosis. Time 43no23:99-100 Je 5 1944.
Review and digest of *Hidden Faces.*

178. METROPOLITAN OPERA HOUSE, NEW YORK. Program [April 6, 1940]. p9, 11 [New York, 1940].
Geological functions of Venusberg, signed: 1939—Salvador Dali.

179. MILLER, HENRY V. [Review of L'Age d'or.] New Review 1:157-9 My 1931.

180. Monte Carlo and the ballet. 2il Vogue p78 Je 15 1938.
Includes color plate for the ballet *Tristan Fou,* and sketch.

181. MORENO VILLA, JOSÉ. Nuevos artistas. Primera exposición de la Sociedad de artistas ibéricos. 3il Revista de Occidente 9no25:80-91 Jy-Ag-S 1925.
Un géometra: Salvador Dali, p86-8.

182. MORSE, A. REYNOLDS. Dream world of Dali. 7il Art in America 33:110-26 Jy 1945.
Includes bibliography, especially references to newspapers and magazines, reproductions and sketches, etc.

182a. NADEAU, MAURICE. Histoire du surréalisme. p209-19 Paris, Editions du Seuil, 1945.

183. Name calling. Art Digest 16no6:3 D 15 1941.
Summary of Louis Guglielmi's reply to Walter Quirt (bibl 198).

184. Napoleon's nose & other objects. 1il Time 46 no22:77 N 26 1945.
Review of Bignou exhibition.

185. NEW BURLINGTON GALLERIES, LONDON. The international surrealist exhibition, Thursday June 11th to Saturday, July 4th, 1936. 32p [London, Women's Printing Society, 1936].
Preface by André Breton. Nos.60-71, and objects, by Salvador Dali.

186. New York criticism: fashionable and very disputed. Art Digest 9no5:14 D 1 1934.

187. New York as seen by the super-realist artist, M. Dali. American Weekly p3 F 24 1935.
With sketches specially prepared for this Sunday section of the New York Journal-American.

188. NEW YORK. MUSEUM OF MODERN ART. Fantastic art, dada, surrealism. Edited by Alfred H. Barr, Jr. and Georges Hugnet. 2d.ed. New York, The Museum of Modern Art, 1937 (c1936).

189. ———————— [Release, January 10, 1935: lecture by Dali on surrealist painting, paranoiac images] 1p [New York, The Museum, 1935].

190. ———————— What is modern painting? By Alfred H. Barr, Jr. p32-3 1il New York, The Museum of Modern Art, 1943. (Introductory series to the modern arts.2.)

———————— See also bibl 213.

191. NICHOLS, D. Ah! madness. Art Digest 13:26 S 1939.
   Reply to Dali's manifesto (bibl 61).

192. Open secret. 1il(por) Newsweek 21no2:62,64 Ja 11 1943.
   Review of *The secret life of Salvador Dali.*

193. ORWELL, GEORGE. Dickens, Dali and others; studies in popular culture. p170-84 New York, Reynal & Hitchcock, 1946.
   Essay titled *Benefit of clergy* originally published in the *Saturday book,* Hutchinson, 1944.

194. PAYRÓ, JULIO E. Pintura moderna, 1800-1940. p209-13 1il Buenos Aires, Editorial Poseidon, 1942.

195. "The persistence of memory"—a surrealist work, a puzzle to visitors at the Art Institute of Chicago. Weekly News Letter (Art Institute of Chicago) S 8 1934.

196. PETITE ANTHOLOGIE POÉTIQUE DU SURRÉALISME. Introduction par Georges Hugnet. p74-82 3il (por) Paris, Editions Jeanne Bucher, 1934.
   Extracts from *Le grand masturbateur, Babaouo, L'amour et la mémoire.*

197. PROCTOR, JAMES and GOODE, GERALD. [Press releases for Dream of Venus pavilion at the World's Fair.] [New York, 1939?].
   Data from releases partly summarized in Art Digest 13:12 My 1 1939.

198. QUIRT, WALTER. Wake over surrealism: with due respect to the corpse. Pinacotheca 1:2-3 D 1941.
   Excerpts printed in *Dali a fascist?* Art Digest 16no5:6, 14 D 1 1941.

199. READ, HERBERT, ed. Surrealism. Contributions by André Breton, Hugh Sykes Davies, Paul Eluard, Georges Hugnet. p74,79,240-2,251 4il London, Faber & Faber, 1936.

200. REID, ALEX. AND LEFEVRE, LTD., LONDON. Salvador Dali, June-July 1936 [4]p 1il [The Gallery, 1936].
   Exhibition catalog, with frontispiece drawing by Dali.

201. RILEY, MAUDE KEMPER. Salvador Dali and our day. Limited Edition no6:5 D 1945.

202. ROUSE, PARKE, JR. Spiders—that's what fascinates Dali most about Virginia. 6il (2por) Richmond Times-Dispatch Ap 6 1941.

203. RIU, FIDEL. El cas Dali. Ciutat 2no15:190 O-D 1927.

204. ROBIN, PIERRE. Les conférences littéraires: Dali Inquisitions 1:51-2 Je 1936.

205. S————, W————. Australia's most important exhibition. 1il Art in Australia 3d series no77:17-18,39 N 1939.
   The Melbourne Herald exhibition.

205a. Salvador Dali a can Dalmau. Gaseta de les Arts 4no65:7 Ja 15 1927.

206. Salvador Dali among the muses: the seven lively arts surrealised. The Sketch 202no2622:154-5 Mr 21 1945.

207. Salvador Dali goes to Hollywood. 2il Theatre Arts 29no3:176-7 Mr 1945.
   The Selznick production *Spellbound,* based on Francis Beeding's "The House of Dr. Edwardes," for which Dali made sketches and oils.

207a. SAN LAZZARO, G. DI. Cinquant' anni di pittura moderna in Francia. 1il p127-32 Roma, Stabilimenti Danesi, 1945.

208. SARGEANT, WINTHROP. Dali; an excitable Spanish artist, now scorned by his fellow surrealists, has succeeded in making deliberate lunacy a paying proposition. 11il(por) Life 19no13:63-6, 68 S 24 1945.

209. SETON, MARIE. S. Dali + 3 Marxes =. 5il Theatre Arts 23no10:734-40 O 1939.
   With illustrations from "a series of drawings made by Salvador Dali as the basis for a script for the Marx brothers."

210. SKIRA, ALBERT [PUBLISHER] Salvador Dali: 42 eaux-fortes et 30 dessins pour Les Chants de Maldoror. Exposition organisée par Les Editions Albert Skira aux Quatre Chemins . . . du 13 au 25 juin 1934. [4]p [Paris, 1934].
   Invitation, p2-4 of which is Dali's essay *L'Angélus de Millet.* Translated by Samuel Putnam in The New Hope 2no4:10,12,24 Ag 1934.

211. SOBY, JAMES THRALL. After Picasso. p106-12 6il New York, Dodd, Mead and Company, 1935.

212. ——————— The light fantastic show. 3il Town and Country 91no4171:68-71, 166 D 1936.

213. ——————— Paintings, drawings, prints; Salvador Dali. 87p including plates New York, The Museum of Modern Art, 1941.
  The plates and supplementary lists of Dali's works, p33-84, constitute a catalog of an exhibition held at the Museum of Modern Art November 19-January 11. Bibliography by Beaumont Newhall, p85-7.

214. SOYER, RAPHAEL. Salvador Dali at the Bignou gallery. New Masses 58no1:26-7 Ja 1 1946.

214a. Speaking of pictures . . . Dali paints the seven lively arts. 8il(por) Life 18no1:4-6 Ja 1 1945.
  Paintings commissioned by Billy Rose for his production *Seven Lively Arts*.

215. SPITZ, JACQUES. La poésie du cinéma [Un chien andalou]. 1il La Revue du Cinéma 3no18:42-8 Ja 1 1931.

216. STEIN, GERTRUDE. Everybody's autobiography. p19-31 New York, Random House, 1937.

217. STEUBEN GLASS, INC., NEW YORK. Collection of designs in glass by twenty-seven contemporary artists. 1il New York, Steuben Glass, Inc. [1940].
  Number 6: Salvador Dali (biographical sketch). Of six pieces executed, one was retained for the permanent collection of the company. (Photographs of the drawings for glass in the possession of Percy Rainford, photographer.)

218. LE SURRÉALISME AU SERVICE DE LA RÉVOLUTION, PARIS. [Documents, 1930-1934.] [Paris, 193?].
  A collection of memorabilia: announcements, catalogs, manuscripts, etc. compiled by the editors of the surrealist periodical. Includes many items signed by or referring to Dali. Bound volume in the library of the Museum of Modern Art.

219. SWING, RAYMOND GRAM. Nativity of a new world. A concept of the outcome of today's travail, created especially for this issue of Esquire by the most discussed of all living painters, Salvador Dali. 1il(col) Esquire 18no6: 43 D 1942.
  Brief comment on double-spread color reproduction facing the text.

219a. TAUBES, FREDERIC. You don't know what you like. p153-61 New York, Dodd, Mead & Company, 1942.

220. TÉRIADE, E. Emancipation de la peinture 1il Minotaure no3-4:18, 20 1933.
  Includes comment by Dali: "Si je dois m'exprimer brièvement sur les questions du 'modèle' . . ."

221. THOMPSON, H. G. If you were in New York. Arts and Decoration 42:46-7 Mr 1935.
  Note on Dali's lecture at the Museum of Modern Art.

222. TORRE, GUILLERMO DE. El salón al fondo del lago o la obra de Dalí. Arte no2:8-15 Je 1933.

223. UTRILLO, MAURICE. Sobre un premio ganado por el pintor Salvador Dali. Gaceta de Bellas Artes 25:37 D 1934.

224. Vogue's 3 man show [Dali, Chirico, Tchelitchew]. 1il(col) Vogue p82-3 Mr 15 1937.

225. WATT, A. Dali à Londres. Beaux-Arts p1 N 30 1934.

226. ——————— Salvador Dali. New Statesman and Nation 8:264-5 S 1 1934.

227. We take off our hat to—Salvador Dali. 7il The Sketch 196no2548:280-1 My 20 1942.

228. WEINSTOCK, CLARENCE. The man in the balloon. Art Front 3no2:8-10 Mr 1937.
  Reply to Dali's statement on Aragon (bibl 70).

229. WILENSKI, REGINALD HOWARD. Modern French painters. p282-3,286,309,314,320-1,324-5,368 New York, Reynal & Hitchcock, 1940.

230. WILSON, EDMUND. Salvador Dali as a novelist. New Yorker 20no20:61, 62, 65 Jy 1 1944.

231. WOOLLCOTT, ALEXANDER. Shouts and murmurs: the wonder book. New Yorker 9no8:34 Ap 8 1933.
  Comment on the film L'Age d'Or.

232. WOLFE, BERTRAM. [The secret life of Salvador Dali—a review.] New York Herald Tribune Book Review p2 D 27 1942.

233. WOOLF, SAMUEL JOHNSON. Dali's doodles come to town. 2il New York Times Magazine p11, 16 Mr 12 1939.
  Includes quotations from interview with Dali.

234. Written by a madman—illustrated by a "super-realist." 5il American Weekly p8 D 16 1934.
  Dali's illustrations for *Les Chants de Maldoror,* and paintings at Julien Levy reviewed for the Sunday section of the New York Journal-American.

235. BRETON, ANDRÉ. Le revolver à cheveux blancs. Paris, Editions des Cahiers Libres, 1932.
Etching by Dali in each of 10 copies printed on Japan paper.

236. ————— Second manifeste du surréalisme. Frontispiece de Salvador Dali. Paris, Editions Kra, 1930 (Club des Soixante. 1).
Edition of 110 copies, 60 "sur velin annam." Frontispiece colored "au pochoir."

237. ————— and ELUARD, PAUL. L'Immaculée conception. Paris, Corti, 1930.
Nos 1-111, of an edition of 2111 copies, include an engraving (frontispiece) by Dali.

237a. CERVANTES SAAVEDRA, MIGUEL DE. Don Quixote. [Illustrated by Salvador Dali] New York, Random House [1946?] (Illustrated Modern Library Series).
Planned for publication late this year, with 40 drawings, of which 10 will be in color.

238. CHAR, RENÉ. Artine. Paris, Editions Surréalistes, 1930.
Nos 1-30, of an edition of 185 copies, include an engraving by Dali.

239. CREVEL, RENÉ. Dali; ou, L'anti-obscurantisme. 30p plus 10 plates. Paris, Corti, 1932.
An original drawing by Dali in 15 copies on Japan paper.
DALI, SALVADOR. L'Age d'or. See bibl 101.

240. ————— Conquest of the irrational. New York, Julien Levy, 1935.
Special edition on Holland paper, 35 French and 35 English copies, containing an original drawing by Dali. Printed by Maison Ramiot of Paris.
————— Hidden faces. See bibl 68.
————— La femme visible. See bibl 66.
————— The secret life of Salvador Dali. See bibl 96.

241. [DUCASSE, ISADORE.] Les chants de Maldoror [par] Comte de Lautréamont. Paris, Albert Skira Editions, 1934.
Edition of 210 copies each containing 42 etchings by Dali (30 plates hors-texte). Copies 1-40 issued with a suite of prints; copies I-X (hors commerce) reserved for the artist and collaborators.

242. ELUARD, PAUL. Nuits partagées. Avec deux dessins par Salvador Dali. Paris, Editions G.L.M., 1935.

243. FOIX, J. V. Conte de Nadal. [2] illustraciones de Salvador Dali. L'Amic de les Arts 1no9:10-1 D 1926.

244. HUGNET, GEORGES. Onan. Paris, Editions Surréalistes, 1934.
Nos 1-50, of an edition of 250 copies, include an original etching.

245. JAMES, EDWARD. Trois sécheresses. Minotaure no8:53-6 1936.
Illustrated with 4 drawings by Dali.
LAUTRÉAMONT, COMTE DE. See bibl 241.

246. PERÉT, BENJAMIN. De derrière les fagots. Eau-forte de Salvador Dali. Paris, Editions des Cahiers Libres, 1934.
Reference from contemporary advertisement. (No illustration in trade edition.)

247. SANDOZ, MAURICE. Fantastic memories. Illustrations by Salvador Dali. Garden City, N. Y., Doubleday Doran and Company, 1944.
Colored book-jacket and 24 drawings.

248. ————— The maze. Illustrations by Dali. Garden City, N. Y., Doubleday, Doran and Company, 1945.
Colored book-jacket and 13 drawings.

249. VIOLETTE NOZIÈRES. Par André Breton, René Char, Paul Eluard [et al]. Dessins de Arp, Victor Brauner, Salvador Dali [et al]. Paris, Editions Nicolas Flamel, 1933.
Includes "portrait paranoïaque" by Dali. 10 copies on Holland paper issued with a suite of signed drawings.

ADVERTISEMENTS, DESIGNS, SKETCHES

Backdrop for the ballet Bacchanale. Color reproduction: The Studio Ap-My 1943.
Backdrop for the ballet Sentimental Colloquy. Color reproduction: Vogue D 15 1944.
Backdrop for the ballet Tristan Fou. Color reproduction: Vogue D 15 1944.
Costume designs for Sentimental Colloquy: Harper's Bazaar O 1938.
Drawings for Bryan Hosiery. Advertisements: Vogue My 15 1944, S 1 1944, O 15 1945.
Free French Relief Calendar. Drawing 1942.
Invitation to Surrealist Night Del Monte, 1941.
Minotaure cover, no8 1936.
New York World's Fair pavilion. Sketch for Dream of Venus: Town and Country Je 1939.
Schiaparelli advertisement. "Shocking radiance" perfume: Harper's Bazaar O 1943.
Vogue cover, Je 1 1939, Ap 1 1944.

This is a representative list, exclusive of numerous references in the bibliography proper. For more complete documentation, see citations by Morse (bibl 182), the Frick Library portfolio (bibl 126), and references in the Art Index (H. W. Wilson Co., N. Y.).